This One Time at the Bar...

True Stories from a Bouncer

RICK JAKEN

Fulton Books
Meadville, PA

Published by Fulton Books 2024

ISBN 979-8-89221-106-2 (paperback)
ISBN 979-8-89221-107-9 (digital)

Printed in the United States of America

This book is dedicated to anyone who has ever felt
the need to drown their sorrows in the bottom of
a bottle and escape their life for a little while or
just wanted to blow some steam off and have fun.
It is especially dedicated to the wonderful
staff at the bars I worked at, including
Larry and Eddie
The HBIC
8-Ball
Snow White, Cute Cathy, Princess,
Baby Gail, Sunshine
Boots, Ross, and Wille
Nachos
Wax
And Lucy's mom, for giving me the courage
to go through with publishing this.

Contents

Prologue

For some, turning twenty-one is a magical moment. Finally, after watching all these movies, television shows, and their peers showcase the amazing nights that could be had at bars, they would be willing participants. Well, I wasn't much different, except for the fact that I was already frequenting a local establishment for the better part of a year before legally being allowed. The nights at the bar were filled with excitement and young adult shenanigans, but lost on me was the greater picture. It wasn't until a year later that the world of pubs fully opened itself up to me. For the next eleven years, I would work as a bouncer. Some refer to the position as a door-guy, security, or simply as staff. Whichever moniker you choose to label it, the responsibility was the same. It was my job to ensure that things ran smoothly.

My first years were spent working at the bar where I was a regular, the one that I was going to illegally. George, the owner, was mad at me when he found out but quickly forgave me. I had never brought friends with me, and I was always respectful. One night, after I was legally allowed to be there, the crowd was abnormally rambunctious. I was not yet employed there and was having a few drinks. A group of already inebriated men came in and immediately started causing issues. George and the bartenders were visibly distraught, and I started getting uneasy. When they sat next to me at the bar, I decided that I was going to leave after I finished. My plans changed slightly when the leader of the drunks tried starting a conversation with the person on the other side of me. It quickly went from friendly to anger in a flash. A fight broke out, and I was caught in the middle. Forgetting that the drunk guy had friends, I turned to confront him. I was met with a barstool to the face. An explosion of pain coursed through my head, and tears filled my eyes. I don't remember much after that until the emergency room at the hospital. George had come to the hospital to check on me. He said he had never seen anyone look so angry. His fear was from the toothless smile I had on my face, blood dripping from my mouth, as I tore through the drunkards. He offered me the job on the spot, and for the next two years, I faithfully spent my weekend nights manning the door.

When that establishment closed, I thought that was the end of my time as a bouncer. Almost a year passed before I got another job. That *audition* was a little different. I was invited to the dive bar that will be the setting for most of the stories that follow by a good friend of mine. It was a quaint little place, but the attraction was this old-timer who ran the karaoke. He was a hoot! It wasn't long until I became a regular attendee on Friday and Saturday nights. As usual, I befriended some of the people, and before I knew it, everyone knew my name. One night, I arrived a little later than normal, and one of my friends was a little shaken up. The night before, he had approached a girl he was interested in. Her boyfriend didn't like that and confronted him in the parking lot, pinning him against a car and threatening him. He told the story, and I could see how scared he was. Later that night, I went to the bathroom, and when I returned to the room, I noticed my friend had slunk into the corner. When I asked him what was wrong, he nodded to a guy and girl at another pool table and said he was the one from the previous night. I turned around and walked over, apparently smiling the whole time. I told this guy that if he ever touched my friend again, I would end him and then calmly returned to our table. The bouncer on staff had started making his way over when he saw me approach but stopped when nothing happened. The bouncer came over and said he had never seen the bully be shaken like that. He asked if I wanted a job, and I said I would think about it. We exchanged numbers, and the next day, I called him and accepted. For nine years, I worked as the bouncer at that establishment. Like most who start in the profession at a younger age, I was cocky. It was my way or the highway. For some reason, young men often feel they must prove themselves as tough, and I learned quickly that there were more effective ways to deal with those situations. It's a little funny, but I actually credit the movie *Roadhouse* with my thought shift. Patrick Swayze's character had a philosophy that was fantastic. I would eventually use the movie as my training video when hiring new security staff—no joke.

My role expanded after the first year there, and before long, it became a full-time job. I would spend most of my nights learning the ins and outs of the business. For nine years, I spent five nights a week working. As time passed, I would notice different things about the bar. There were four distinct crowds. For lack of better terminology, I will refer to them as shifts. The first shift was comprised mainly of retired tradesmen and typically arrived shortly after opening and stayed until around 5:00 p.m. The second shift was the working-class stiffs who stopped for a quick beer after their job to wind down or avoid the nagging wife as some would claim. The same group of guys every day would come in and drink until they were summoned home. At about 10:00 p.m., the third shift would start meandering in. These were the typical young people looking to blow off steam, find the love of the night, or just get obliterated. Most of the issues in our bar would stem from this shift. Young people full of energy and angst can get unruly when adding alcohol to the mix. I imagine dealing with toddlers is a very similar situation. The *swing* shift didn't have a set time or day when they would come, and they were comprised of the local 1 percent motorcycle club in the area. They were the most volatile, and welcomed at times, group that frequented our establishment.

The perspective in a setting like that changes when you are an outside observer. Years spent watching people in a bar while remaining completely sober lent to some interesting scenarios. What follows is a compilation of some of the things I witnessed from my stool by the door. Some of them will be really funny, and some of them will be sad. All of them are true. You may even relate to some of the instances that occurred. A lot of them will be unbelievable. If I had not witnessed them firsthand, I wouldn't believe them either. Whatever you may glean from them, my hope is that they are enjoyable in some manner. Without further ado, *This One Time at the Bar...*

1

Cake

We all have met that one person at a bar who just grates on so many people that it almost becomes a joke. If you aren't familiar with being a bar regular, you can easily substitute that person for someone in your chosen hobbies or pastimes. Are you an avid sports fan? Then this is the guy who knows everything about your favorite team and espouses insignificant stats as if he were an employee of Sports Trackers R Us, except he is wrong nearly all the time. Generally speaking, they are nice enough people; there is just something that puts the room on edge when they enter. More often than not, they have nicknames given to them by the other regulars, but it is only referenced secretly or rarely, if ever, in front of the offender. Well, this is the story of how one regular patron of the bar got his nickname, and boy is it a tasty one. Let me introduce you to Cake.

The day started off normally for a Sunday afternoon during football season in the Midwest. The Chicago Bears were playing some team or another, and a small crowd had gathered at the bar. Sundays were a fantastic day for me during this time of the year. Fall is by far my favorite season, and this day did not disappoint. A chill in the air suggested that winter was around the corner, and the sun was shining—like I said, "Standard autumn day." Sunday football can be religion-like in this part and, I'm sure, other parts, of the country. Folks gather at homes and eateries alike to celebrate their teams' victories on the gridiron. Since the inception of Fantasy Football, it has taken on a new meaning for fans of the sport, me included. I participate in several different leagues with various groups of people. Also, there is the Confidence Pools, Squares, and/or other gambling hobbies the pigskin fans look forward too. It should be noted that I participate in those as well. My goal on Sunday, during football season, is to find an establishment that offers me the largest selection of televised games to keep track of statistics, scores, and injuries. Oh, and it must be relatively quiet. I am not a fan of the Flying Buffalo restaurant because it is overwhelmingly loud at times, and after six hours of partaking in food and adult beverages, my bank account would take a serious hit. Plus, the whole drinking and driving thing is not really something I aspire too. So with all those parameters needed to be met, the establishment I would choose with regularity on Sundays was the one I was employed at six days a week.

As was previously stated, average football Sunday was the epitome of my existence on this most sacred of days. I arrived shortly after the bar opened for business, 10:30 a.m., and made my way to my customary throne. From my perch, I had a view of all the television sets, both doors, and the kitchen. It was directly across from where the bulk of the fans entering were going to sit, which was right in front of the sink. It was placed strategically in a location where the barmaid would have to bend over slightly while cleaning glasses and offer a hint of femininity that most of the male clientele either lacked at home or just enjoyed—no judgment here. Sex sells in this business, and we had the best eye candy in the land! My choice of seat was twofold. First, it offered the bartender a moment of respite when they had to refill my beverage or bring food or really any reason to get away from that gaze for a little while. Second, and the most important, my location was a void. No one liked sitting at the spot I did due to the aforementioned lack of female view. I loved it! I was a solitary man stranded on an island, left to enjoy (or hate) the outcomes on the screens in front of me. Scrap Iron arrived shortly after I did and got the best seat in the house. Remember the rule about nicknames? Well, it isn't always how people get their monikers. Scrap Iron was a retired steel mill worker, and his was a matter of respect. He didn't even enjoy football, but he came every week. Company was his desired interaction. All the patrons obliged him of that want. The roster of watchers was filled just before kickoff, and the festivities were underway.

When halftime rolled around, the crowd was beginning to be well lubricated. Arguments had happened, jokes were told, and a general camaraderie had been established. That was until Steve entered the picture. Here was our guy, the annoying one that everyone just had a disdain for that could only be described as just slightly soured milk. For reference, milk that has just started to turn has a slightly bad smell and a slight bad taste. You could drink it and be fine, but why put yourself through that discomfort? That was Steve in a nutshell. Collectively, the room got up and went outside. Recently, a statewide law banning indoor smoking had been implemented, and those who partook in the nicotine lifestyle had to go outside to indulge their habit. They all went at the same time. The entirety of the mood shifted immediately upon his entrance. Fifteen of the sixteen patrons and the bartender all left for a smoke break. I was the lone person left. Since I was an employee and tended bar two nights a week, I spelled *Princess* so she could join her customers. Steve made an all-too-accurate joke about how nobody liked him as they were exiting the building. A nervous chuckle accompanied by a meek denial went right over his head. Small talk between a bartender and their customers runs a wide range of topics. It is often utilized to gauge a person's feelings or mood. Our job is to listen. I humored his attempt. We exchanged pleasantries, and I offered him his ultralight beer and turned to watch the games. Autopilot engaged, and I barely registered what he was saying. Complimentary nods joined in with inattentive ahas and yeahs as the time crawled on. It felt like hours, days maybe, but it was only about fifteen minutes before the group rejoined us. We all took our positions again and prepared for the second half of the football game.

Steve wasn't inherently a bad guy; there was just an aura surrounding him that was unpleasant. I am positive that he had problems in his life that he was just trying to escape from, like all the others in the room with him, and some part of me believes that he could sense that we didn't enjoy his company. He had recently divorced, his teenagers were ambivalent to his existence, and he worked a middling job at a copy machine company. I know he was there just to be around people who were in similar positions in their own lives, but that hardly mattered to all of us on our sacred day of watching grown men run back and forth with a ball. It was that reason that I didn't move or leave when he inevitably sat next to me. I could see the others smirking and talking in whispers, out of the corner of my eye. It annoyed me to no end, but I could feel the sadness emanating from Steve, so I let him vent.

The games weren't particularly exciting one way or the other, so I let myself listen to him drone on and on. I learned that he had recently lost eighty-five pounds. At that moment, I realized he did! He looked completely different than when I first met him. That is an accomplishment that should be celebrated! However, I was so caught up in avoiding him that I missed that he was trying extremely hard to right his ship. Well, that made me feel like crap, rightfully so. After his divorce, he went into a deep depression and gained a bunch of weight. He, like thousands of people before him, struggled to shed the weight. Changing his diet had a positive effect, as did exercising more. No matter how hard he worked, he just couldn't get over that plateau. Ultimately, he made the decision to get the gastric bypass surgery. What a game changer that was for him! Excitedly, he told me that all the weight started falling off, he was sleeping better, and his overall health improved. I bought him his next round, and when Princess asked what the occasion was, Steve happily recanted his story. She bought him his next round, and the guys in the room cheered his accomplishment, and the chips piled up for him. His smile was only dwarfed by how red his face was, and the rest of the game was more enjoyable than anyone could have expected.

As the afternoon turned into early evening, the crowd grew smaller, and the next crew started funneling in. Princess finished her end-of-day procedures, and when Cute Candy arrived, they had their change of shift meeting. It wasn't really a meeting, but more of a status report of the day's events. As chance would have it, a keg blew right as the switch happened, and since I was there, I took it upon myself to change it. Princess was telling CC that Steve had been there for a little while but only had a couple of beers and that he hadn't been overly annoying. I piped in and said that he had been pleasant to speak with for once. The thing about Steve was he was absolutely enamored with CC. Since bar patronage is a male-dominated demographic, female bartenders deal with constant leering and untoward behaviors. It can be an unfortunate part of the job. Sex sells, am I right? Having recently gotten a boost of confidence from the groups' excitement over his accomplishment, Steve started up a conversation with CC. I was able to overhear what was being said from my watch post, and if I am being honest, it was a little cute.

As the evening progressed, so did Steve's intake of alcohol. It wasn't very long before his face became flushed, and his speech became a little off. The late afternoon games finished, and I settled my bar tab, restocked the coolers for the evening, and excused myself to the bathroom. When I entered the bathroom, there were four people in the bar, not including me. My plan was to go home and shower and nap before I had to come back and work the late shift. When I left the bathroom, there was one patron left, Steve. As I made my way through the bar toward the exit, a sinking feeling came over me. I couldn't leave CC with an increasingly inebriated Steve by herself, could I? When I took my seat, reluctantly, CC came over, placed a drink in front of me, and said, "Thank you." Her eyes, however, screamed, "OMG! OMG! OMG! THANK YOU FOR NOT LEAVING ME ALONE!" I would just have to resign myself to the fact that there was going to be no nap for me today.

A few people came in and out over the next hour, but not enough so that I could comfortably leave. Steve got bolder with his words and at one point said something that made CC extremely uncomfortable. She went into the back to take a break for a minute, and while she was gone, I manned the bar. I told him that what he said had crossed a line and that it might be time for him to go. I could see CC in the backroom wiping tears from her eyes, and that made me boil. I removed his full beer from the bar in front of him and slow-poured it into the sink while not breaking eye contact. For a brief moment, there was a flash of anger in his eyes. I thought that he might want to get physical, but it quickly subsided when I saw fear come across him. He stammered through apologies and asked if he could go say sorry to CC. I handed him his bill, told him to settle up, and that I would let her know. He reluctantly agreed and then said he was going to use the washroom. CC finished her break, and I went back to my seat. The night continued.

Our regular night group made their way to their assigned seats over the next half hour, and the events from earlier quickly faded from our memories. Despite not having a nap, it felt like the night was going to be a good one. One of the guys excused himself and seconds later returned to the bar with eyes wide open and mouth agape. He said, "Ricky, there is a mess you need to clean up in the bathroom," and started laughing. I was furious. I retrieved the cleaning supplies from the closet and made my way to the bathroom thinking that Steve left me a present when he went home earlier. When I opened the door, I was stopped dead in my tracks. The sight before me was incredible. To set this scene, I need to describe the layout of our bathroom. It was a small room with a single sink. There was a regular toilet, and directly opposite was the wall urinal. Two men could use the facilities if they were butt to butt, but if someone were to make a *deposit*, it could only fit one.

I laugh about it now, but at the time, I was immediately concerned. Steve had not gone home, as I had previously thought. There he was, half on the toilet with his pants around his ankles. He leaned forward, passed out in the wall urinal. I reached out with the mop handle to prod him. He was completely out. I kicked a little harder, and he responded with a muffled noise. For those of you who have never viewed a wall urinal before, there is something you should know. In most of these units, at the bottom, is a round tablet to help with the smell and sanitation of the urinal. It is called a urinal cake. Now, if you can do basic math, you are starting to put together these numbers: Steve face-first in urinal, muffled noise, and urinal cake. It was hard to stomach, and I nearly vomited in my mouth. He was apologizing profusely, and every word was muted by the urinal cake that was in his mouth. I helped him up, and together, we got him all put together.

I leaned him up on the wall and ensured him that no one knew he was here and not to be embarrassed. When I entered the main room of the bar, I was met with a burst of laughter from the remaining people. It quickly went away when they sensed the anger that was flowing out of me. I told CC to call a cab and told everyone else to get out for a bit. They initially resisted, but I convinced them I needed a couple of minutes to clean and disinfect and I would buy them all a round. They obliged, and fifteen minutes later, the cab arrived. I helped Steve into the back. I leaned into the driver, gave him the address, said how sorry I was, and gave him a hundred bucks. I reopened the bar and made good on my promise to buy the round. I called my boss and told him what had happened and then went home to shower. When I came back for my shift, the story had quickly spread, and Steve now had a new nickname. From that day forward, he was known as Cake, and to this day, I am sure he has no idea why.

Red Fell Down

For a large portion of my employment at the bar, I wore many hats. First and foremost, I was the head of security. Door-guy, bouncer, cooler, however you wanted to describe it—that was me. Mine was the face you first saw when you entered the building. Second, I was a bartender. I didn't tend on the busy nights, just a couple of days during the week and Sunday nights. My third hat was a janitor's cap. Every day before the bar opened, or after it closed, I would restock the coolers, sweep up the mess, and clean the bathrooms. On the busy nights, I would just stay after hours and clean after everyone went home. Sometimes, mainly on Sundays, I would clean before the bar opened and then hang out for a while to see some people whom I didn't normally interact with. These days were usually calm and peaceful. We didn't get a large group of patrons, and for hours, it was only me and the bartender, Baby Rey. We would have lunch together and fill each other in on the various events in our lives. As most of these stories go, this was not a normal day.

It started off like most other Sundays did. The previous night's crowd was more rambunctious than usual, which meant the cleaning was a little harder. It was before the statewide indoor smoking ban had been implemented. At that time, it was up to the individual counties whether to ban smoking, and we were in between two counties who implemented the ban; our county didn't. It increased our crowd size immensely since people could enjoy their beverages and stay inside while smoking. It also helped that we had been grandfathered into the liquor licensing requirements of operating hours and were open until 4:00 a.m. when most establishments had to close at 2:00 a.m. Every night (morning, I suppose) at 2:00 a.m., we would have a rush of people. They were packed in shoulder to shoulder, and we were probably in violation of some fire code or another. Cigarette butts would be put out on the floor, full ashtrays would be emptied into the corners of the room, and beer bottles and plastic cups rarely made it to the trash receptacles.

The tornado of drunkards from the night prior made cleaning more challenging, and I still hadn't mopped the floors when Baby Rey arrived, and she laughed audibly when she saw the pile of trash bags I had piled up at the exit. Chuckling along with her, I went back to diligently finishing my task. She brought doughnuts and coffee with her, which made the sting of her laughter go away immediately, and before long, I was finished. Previously, I have described to you my nesting area during football season, but during these days, my perch was different. Baby Rey would sit on the stool closest to the bar access, and I would sit right next to her, adjacent to the hot seat. Since it was early spring in the Midwest, the weather was warmer than the last few months, and people were excited for sunshine and tolerable climate. That meant the midfifties in temperature, by the way. On this day, it was unseasonably warm and pushed past the sixty-degree mark. We opened the doors, and all of the sounds of early spring could be heard. There was an unwritten rule regarding playing the jukebox before one o'clock, for some of the old-timers, but we ignored that on Sundays when it was me and Baby Rey. The service that collected the money for the music had shown Baby Rey a function on the remote that allowed us free credits. We would turn the music down and just listen to songs and talk. Sometimes, we would put credits on for the few people who would show up throughout the day.

Riding motorcycles is a popular pastime in our area, and on this bright spring day, the rumbles of bikes could be heard consistently on the streets outside. People were excited to unfurl their hogs and tool about town with their pasty white arms showing from the sleeveless shirts they had been dying to wear since the dreary winter had ceased. It was a welcome sound to me because it signaled the start of softball season, and our conversation turned to the team we were going to field this year. Baby Rey had a crush on our manager, and she had specifically switched to Sundays so she could see him every week—not a bad tactic and one that I use to this day! Thanks to the beautiful weather, the seats remained empty for some time. Eventually, we would hear the rumblings of some big motorcycles, and our first customers would arrive.

Have I mentioned that the bar I worked at was a regular stopping point for a motorcycle club before? No? Well, the local area motorcycle club, MC for short or *biker gang* for the uninitiated, used our tavern as a clubhouse away from home. They were the 1 percent in the area, and for obvious reasons, I won't say which one it was. Let's just say that the *outlaw* Jessie James would have been proud.

Two members of the MC, and their lady friends, joined us that afternoon. We were well acquainted with one another, and when Baby Rey saw them walk through the door, she promptly got them two pitchers of their favorite lager and four glasses. After using the restroom, they made small talk about their ride and went into the backroom to play pool. Red was a stout man with, you guessed it, long red hair. Big Joe wasn't really big, but his name was given to him for his proclivity to drink large cups of coffee, all the time. He literally had a travel mug full of coffee and drank from it while also imbibing his beer. They were regulars and knew us from years of service. I tell people all the time when the 1 percent were in the bar, I never worried about backup, unless they were the ones I needed backup from. On several occasions, Big Joe and Red were around when I was working solo, and things got dicey, and a respect formed between us. An hour or so after they arrived, we got our second group of customers, and when they entered the building, I stopped being a patron and put my bouncer hat on. At the risk of sounding judgmental, these punks were going to be trouble. The old adage of oil and water not mixing is true for a reason because they don't.

Now, the bar itself was situated in a suburb of Chicago, and there was a large urban influence in the area. It pains me to even describe this. The new group that came in fancied themselves as some sort of gang. They adopted the vernacular, clothing, and general lifestyle of what some perceive as *thugs*. I refer to these types of people as posers. Cultural appropriation is a term that is widely used to describe the phenomenon. White middle-class kids who were drawn to the music and images on screens everywhere thought that they were accepted as a part of that lifestyle. I'm all for people enjoying what they want or trying to find commonality in something that they can feel connected to. This wasn't that. They leveraged this behavior into bullying people and would use phrases and terms that are designed to intimidate people. Their attempts to live in a way that large groups of people are forced to live because of oppression, undereducation, and a century's worth of hate disgusted me. They were entering into a domain that they weren't ready for.

After they ordered their beverages, I moved my seat to a vantage point that would allow me to monitor them in the backroom. I knew they were going to play pool, and I knew they were going to pick the table right next to Red and Big Joe. There was a third table, but I knew they were going to purposefully pick the table right next to our guests. I was not disappointed when they set their stuff down. I asked Baby Rey to grab the phone and have it ready if something were to happen. She started to protest but changed her mind when she saw how serious my expression was. Years of watching people, intervening in physical attacks, and caring for the well-being of the establishment and the patrons conditioned me for moments like this. You need to trust your instincts, and you must be prepared for things to go sideways fast. My gut told me that this situation was potentially volatile. Sure, there was a chance that the two groups would coexist peacefully. I just needed to be ready.

It didn't take long before the posers started their antics. The leader struck up a conversation about the bikes outside. Red and Big Joe were short in their answers, and I could feel the tension building. Poser 1 would wait for one of the bikers to line up a shot and then casually interfere, always saying he was sorry. He would bump into the ladies, say he was sorry, and then minutes later bump into one of the men. Round and round it went, and the knot in my stomach grew bigger. Poser 2 asked if the bikers wanted to play a game or two for money. They declined and said they were just here to spend time with the ladies. Poser 3 said something along the lines of, "Yeah, I would be scared too." Big Joe turned around and peacefully confronted him, telling him they weren't here for anything but cold beer and good company. He also told them he didn't appreciate the infantile way they were bumping into them. Poser 1 got loud, and I entered the room. I told them all to calm down and move tables, and they did. I went back into the bar area, and Baby Rey said, "See, no harm, no foul."

My mistake was leaving the room. It was a rookie mistake. No sooner than sitting down, I looked up to see Poser 1 move across the room and hit Red in the back of the head with his pool cue. The stick broke, and the fracas started. Immediately, I yelled at Baby Rey to call 911, and then I went into action. I came around the corner, and Poser 2 and 3 were moving toward Big Joe, and Poser 1 was jumping on Red. I had to act quickly, and when I saw the girls move in to help Big Joe, I went for Poser 1. Red was bleeding profusely from the back of his head, and I grabbed Poser 1's arm right before he started unleashing blows on his dazed opponent. Glasses shattered, and tables toppled as the girls and Big Joe went at it with the other two posers. I grabbed Poser 1 around the neck with my free arm and dragged him off and out into the main room. He turned on me when I let him go but thought better and turned to run out the door. I turned my attention to the remaining combatants. I would much rather deal with males in a bar fight than females for many reasons. Girls are vicious and unrelenting! Scratches and blood were forming on Poser 2's face, and Poser 3 was getting handily beaten by Big Joe. Red started getting up from the floor, and I got between the girls and Poser 2. Poser 3 got out of Big Joe's grip and made his way to the exit, with Poser 2 quickly following.

I retrieved a clean towel for Red's head and then got to cleaning up the mess. Five minutes passed before the police showed up. The whole fight took less than two. Red was sitting on a stool, Big Joe was on the phone, the girls were in the bathroom, and Baby Rey was standing with mouth agape when they arrived. They asked what happened, and Baby Rey started to tell them. Red looked up and interrupted, saying he fell and hit his head on the pool table. Clearly, that was not what happened. My position as the bouncer had brought me familiar with the local law enforcement, and I knew these officers well. They separated me from the group and asked me what had happened. I was in a very difficult position. I couldn't lie to the police, and I didn't want to tell them anything that would anger the 1 percent. So I simply said, "Whatever Red said happened, happened," and that I didn't see what happened because I wasn't officially on duty and in a different room. I knew they knew that I knew that they knew I wasn't being truthful, but that was my only option at the time. They took down all the information and said they would be back for the camera footage later. Big Joe and Red nodded at me, and then they left. The rest of the day proceeded normally.

Sunday night wasn't extremely busy, so I decided that I was going to clean up the next morning. I showed up two hours before opening, and when I was done, there was still a half hour before Princess would arrive. I sat at the bar with a soda and turned on the jukebox. Have you ever been in or near an earthquake? How about a tornado? In an earthquake, you can feel the ground shaking, and a tornado sounds like a freight train. About fifteen minutes before the bartender's arrival, I felt the ground shaking. Then a low rumble turned into a cacophony. I slowly moved to the front door. When I looked out the window, my heart sank, and my breath stopped. I could feel my knees start to wobble. Turning into the parking lot were one hundred motorcycles. It may have been less; it may have been more, but it was loud, and the ground was shaking, and it felt like there were one hundred. Leading the cavalcade was Sponge, the president of the local chapter of the 1 percent. Behind him were Red and Big Joe. Behind them was a sea of bikers.

They approached the door and motioned for me to unlock it. I couldn't stop myself. I watched from outside my body as I reached down, turned the lock, and pushed the door open. I saw Princess pull into her parking spot and just stare at me. Sponge dominated the conversation. He wanted to know who the guys in the fight were, and I told him, as truthfully as possible, that I only knew their first names. I really only had that information. He stared through my soul, and it was one of only a handful of times in my life I was frightened. He turned and looked at Red and asked him if he believed me. Red said (I will never forget this), "Ricky is good people. He wouldn't lie to you, Sponge. He knows what would happen if he did." Sponge smiled and thanked me, and as he turned around, I took my first breath in what seemed like forever. The thing I did next still haunts me to this day. I couldn't stop myself from blurting out that I may not know their last names but I know where they hang out. Red said, "See… good people."

The rumble was even louder as they pulled out of the parking lot. Princess exited her car and approached me. Shaking still, I held the door open for her. She chuckled as she passed me and said that I sure do have a way with people. The police came by not long after that, and I informed them that the cameras were not on during the time of the *accident*. I wasn't lying. At some point, the cameras were shut off—lucky break, I guess. Over the next few days, I listened for rumors but didn't hear anything. Sunday came, and Big Joe and Red showed up with their lady friends and went about their business, as if nothing happened. We didn't talk about it. Baby Rey didn't say anything. Every time the door opened that day, we held our breath. The posers never showed up. Come to think of it. I never saw them again.

The *Boat*!

The biggest attraction at our bar, besides the sometimes-cold beer and smoky atmosphere, was the DJ we employed four nights a week for karaoke. You read that right, four nights a week. From Thursday night to Sunday, budding stars from across the land visited to live out their rock star fantasies. 8-Ball was the name of the DJ, and he was as entertaining, if not more, than the singers who would stand on his stage. When I started working there, he was sixty-three years old. Our friendship grew strong over the next almost decade, and a mutual respect formed that I have rarely had since. In the age of digital content everywhere, he stood by his archaic CD player, and his sidekick, Marty Q, dutifully made copies of karaoke discs and numbered them all. He took care of 8-Ball's technical needs. Always topped with a baseball cap and a beer and a cigarette never far from his hands, he would blare into the microphone and bring smiles to everyone in the place. I could write a book about the man, and maybe one day will, but for now, we'll settle for a set of days that were eye-opening.

In order to drum up business on days that aren't considered high-volume days, bars will deploy different tactics. Some will have bands, some will have trivia nights, and some will have the phenomenon known as karaoke. Our pub was of the latter variety, and we leaned heavily into it. Sunday nights, for most tap rooms, are a night of recovery. Crowds are not as plentiful, and there is a calmness, most of the time. The karaoke crowd on Sunday night was usually the same fifteen people singing the same songs. When 8-Ball would call them up on the stage by their name, I would know exactly what song was going to be song next. It was enjoyable. We would add themes to the nights sometimes, which made for some fun nights. It's how I found out that I do a pretty wicked rendition of "Santa Baby." It was decided one night that we were going to add a raffle to Sunday nights with a cash prize. 8-Ball would add ten dollars to the pot, and the bar would match it. If your number got called, you got a chance to win by drawing miniature billiard balls from a sack. If you pulled the 8-Ball, you won the money; if you pulled the cue ball, you won a free drink. There would be three pulls. If there wasn't a winner, the money would roll over to the next week.

Our adventure starts on a night when there hadn't been a winner for fifteen weeks, and the kitty was up to $300. Word of mouth spread, and the crowd was as big as a regular Friday night. Who wouldn't want a chance to win? All you had to do to enter was buy a drink or sing a song. Early on in the night, 8-Ball declared that someone was going to win and, to celebrate, we were going to go to the riverboat casino. He liked to frequent the boat to play blackjack, and I would accompany him mainly because he didn't drive. Throughout the night, he would announce over the mic that we were going to the boat. I had the next couple of days off, and my roommate decided that he was going to take Monday off and join us. As predicted, someone won the jackpot, and a cacophony of cheers rose. 8-Ball yelled and chanted into the mic, "The boat, the boat, the BOAT, boat, boat, boat!" The bar emptied quickly after the prize, and it wasn't long until we were back to a regular Sunday night. I had a little help closing up and cleaning, and we headed out to the riverboat.

For legal purposes, every twenty-four hours, the boat had to close for a couple of hours. We would have two hours before shutdown, which was perfect. I already had it planned: breakfast after I dropped 8-Ball home and then a long day of sleep. I don't like gambling, so usually, I would just watch him do his thing. Roomie joined him at the table that night, and both did surprisingly well. The announcement came over the speakers that the boat was closing soon, and my companions cashed out. On the way back to the car, 8-Ball suggested we go get something to eat. Reluctantly, I agreed. There was mischievousness in his eyes, and I knew where, and why, he was about to suggest the destination to satiate our hunger. There was another bar in town that opened 8:00 a.m. and served pretty good, and cheap, breakfast. However, it was only 6:00 a.m. My suggestion was to go hang out at my house until the other bar opened, but they both knew that my plan was to go home and fall asleep. It was decided that we would go to 8-Ball's house and have a couple of drinks in the garage while we waited. I hadn't had a drink at all up to this point. I was the designated driver from the night before, and 8-Ball and Roomie had been drinking all night long. While we were passing time until breakfast, Roomie struck up a conversation about 8-Ball's legendary exploits. We heard rumors of these epic binge nights that he would go on with people. I had witnessed some of these because they usually started on Saturday night and ended on Monday morning, and I would be the person who would retrieve him from our bar to bring him home. I could feel the excitement building in Roomie. With a grin on his face, he called his work and said he was going to take the next two days off. He hung up, turned to me, and said, "Well, Ricky, looks like we are about to become legends."

When we arrived for breakfast, the bartender welcomed us with open arms. Before we sat at the bar, 8-Ball's beer was already at his customary seat. We ordered food, and I ordered a soda to drink. The food was delicious, the company was good, and eventually, I broke down and ordered a screwdriver. I didn't drink as heavily as the others, and in the two and a half hours we were there, I had only two drinks. At ten-thirty, we moved locations. I parked in the back, which will be funnier later, and we proceeded into our bar, where we were greeted by a smile and an "Oh no, here's trouble!" from Princess. The rest of the afternoon we were treated as a sideshow. People would come in, and they would call others to come and witness the spectacle that was ongoing. I have a weird habit when I get a little tipsy. See, I have an unnaturally warm body temperature, and as more alcohol gets consumed, my temperature goes up. I also have an aversion to wearing pants. At some point in the day, I removed my pants and was sitting in the bar with nothing but my boxers on. People would go to the jukebox to play a song, and I would walk up to them to see what they were going to play. Laughter would erupt, and the patron at the music box would laugh along with the crowd—good times. There is a picture floating around somewhere of me in my boxers in the back parking lot helping someone fix their truck. The other shop owners would come out and see me, laugh, and fetch other people to watch what was going on. I was oblivious to the joke.

Eventually, the day turned to night, shift change came, and a whole new crowd came to join us. Roomie and I were fading quickly, and we decided that maybe we weren't cut out for an 8-Ball Binge Trip. 8-Ball, however, was a machine. He kept drinking and laughing and drinking. Word of our trip spread through town, and people from other bars started showing up for the festivities. It reached Roomie's dad, and he eventually showed up. We stayed at our bar until midnight, at which point it was decided we would end there and go home. Wait, that didn't happen. You guessed it, we went to *the boat*! I had sobered up a little by then and had my pants back on, but I was still in no shape to drive. Luckily, we had many targets to choose from. Roomie's dad turned us down but gave us $20 each to play slot machines at the boat. Relentlessly we tried to coerce others into joining us on the grand adventure, but we failed. It looked like we were finally finished. That was until a cab pulled up outside, and the HBIC (head bitch in charge; she'll be in a couple of stories coming up) kicked us out with a smile. The adventure continues! Roomie fell asleep on the drive, 8-Ball gave the cabbie some guff, and I just stared out the window and contemplated my life choices.

We were all still in the previous day's clothes, and when we walked into the casino, the security in the front laughed. They recognized us and escorted us (I think as a joke) to 8-Ball's preferred table. Roomie disappeared somewhere, and I took my $20 to the nearest slot machine. I had never sat at a slot machine in my life before. The screen in front of me had so many numbers and buttons that a sober Rick would have had a hard time figuring it out. I put the money in it and stared at the screen. A little old lady sitting next to me said something to me and pointed at a button. I nodded, smiled, pressed the button, and pulled the lever. An explosion of lights and a blustering of bells and ringing made me freeze. The lady next to me scowled and said something about how she should have sat there. I stared at the machine, seemingly for hours, and had no idea what to do. Someone from the casino approached me and turned the machine off, gathered my ticket, and escorted me to the cage. I was at the casino for five minutes and won $2,000. This was going to be a good night. I bought the drinks for the rest of the night. We stayed until almost closing time. We were about a half hour away from the end, when my proclivity for pants-less existence crept back up. In the middle of the casino floor, I removed my bottoms and was all but tackled by security—no harm, no foul. People were laughing, pointing. Roomie tried to get a picture, but he wasn't fast enough, and I was escorted out. As luck would have it, our cabbie was sitting outside waiting for a new fare. We piled in and headed off.

Suggestions of where our next destination were quickly squelched when I came up with the best idea ever. I had a pocketful of cash and the keys to a bar and was just drunk enough to think this was a good idea. We headed back to our bar. I pulled out a pad of paper and made sure to keep track of every drink we had. 8-Ball said that it was nice working with me and that I was surely going to be fired. I shrugged it off and proceeded to turn the jukebox on and fill everyone up. About fifteen minutes later, the phone rang. We all looked at the camera and waved to my boss, who was in Florida for the offseason, on the many cameras. I answered the phone, preparing to be chewed out. He simply said, "Make sure you pay for everything and restock before Princess got there." I hung the phone up and turned to 8-Ball with an enormous grin.

The three of us skipped out on breakfast that morning. We exchanged stories, but mainly we just listened to 8-Ball talk. He had an interesting tale. He was from Minnesota and played baseball. He earned a contract with the Chicago White Sox, as a pitcher, in the sixties and faced some pretty hefty competition. Check him out; his name was Martin Nyquist. Beneath his chronicle was a sadness. He was married and divorced a couple of times and had children from all of them. He didn't say it, but I finally could understand why he didn't want to go home. He was lonely. He made mistakes like the rest of us, but in the end, he just wanted to be loved. I'm glad for the people who were able to be there for him when he finally left this rock. He was loved dearly.

My pants were already off when Princess arrived. Immediately, she got on the phone with the boss when I told her he said it was okay that we were there. People started pouring in when it was announced that we were still going strong. By noon, we had recruited a couple of others to join us, including a driver for the day. We settled up our tab and decided we were going to go to the breakfast place. With eight people in tow, we arrived to cheers and laughter. We ordered some food and made our way out on to the patio. Others from this place joined us when they heard that we were in the middle of a two-day bender out of sheer disbelief. One of the regulars from our bar had tagged along. He wasn't the most well-liked guy in the bar, but we didn't care. After the amount of alcohol we imbibed over the last twenty-four-plus hours and the lack of rest, it was a feat that tempers didn't flare up before they did. 8-Ball and Unfriendly started exchanging japes at one another, and eventually Unfriendly snapped. He made an aggressive move at 8-Ball, and my instincts took over. I intercepted him and, with a single shove, sent his ass overhead, over the railing into the bushes. The kerfuffle was over as quickly as it started, and within a minute or two, we were all laughing about it, sharing drinks. We spent the rest of the afternoon playing horseshoes and drinking. Our ride eventually said they needed to go home. We piled inside their car and made our triumphant return to our bar. It was 6:00 p.m. on Tuesday evening. We had started on Sunday.

The laughter that greeted us the previous evening was not there when we arrived this time. HBIC was leery at serving us, rightfully so, and informed me she had heard about our shenanigans earlier in the other bar. I was warned that if my pants came off at all, I would be cut off, 8-Ball was told he couldn't start anything with anyone, and Roomie was told he couldn't fall asleep on the bar. All three of these requirements would fail before the night was over. We were well-behaved all night—well, almost all night.

At 10:00 p.m., the wheels started falling off our caravan. Roomie was the first to fail and fell asleep at the bar. HBIC called his dad, and he was shipped home. When they left the bar, he received a standing ovation. About an hour later, I came back from the bathroom sans pants, and my excursion of libations ended. Twenty minutes later, 8-Ball and Unfriendly were back at each other, and this time, it ended with a punch from the old-timer. True to her word, HBIC kicked us out. She called us a cab and sent us home. We ended the night at 8-Ball's house in the garage, finishing the last of his beer. We were awakened by 8-Ball's roommate, Big Carl (he'll be in at least one more story). Looking down, I noticed that I still wasn't wearing pants, and I had no idea where they were. 8-Ball went into shower, and Big Carl went back to bed. I had no phone or pants and was a mile from my truck, so I started walking. It didn't take very long, and when I reached my destination, I realized I didn't have my keys. The bar didn't open for another hour. I hopped into the bed of the truck and fell asleep. Hours later, I awoke and entered the bar. The people inside laughed at me, and I didn't make eye contact with any of them. Princess put a plastic cup of water on the counter. Then she placed my folded pants, phone, and keys in front of me, along with my bar tab from the night before. I settled up, thanked her, and left.

I never went on another legendary 8-Ball bender again. I also never put money in a slot machine either. The bond that I had with 8-Ball grew strong after that, and I tried my hardest to never let him feel alone. One of the hardest things that I went through when I left the business was making a con-scious choice to not keep in touch with those that I had spent nine years with. Even harder was not keep-ing in touch with 8-Ball. When he passed a couple of years ago, multiple people reached out to me. I was able to say my goodbyes, and I even set foot in the bar for the first time in years. It was as if I had never left. We regaled each other with stories of our time with him. It was sad and happy all at the same time. A picture came up during the slide show of his memorial. There we were in all our glory: 8-Ball with his cigarette and beer, Roomie with half-open eyes, and me with a giant smile and no pants. The crowd burst into laughter, and together they chanted, "The boat, the boat, the BOAT, BOAT, BOAT, BOAT!" We were legends.

4

Prospects

Fights, misunderstandings, and kerfuffles are inevitable in the bar business. Most of the time, it is a minor nuisance that can be dealt with without violence erupting. However, there are moments when things escalate to more than a scrum. It is important that you remain calm and aware in these situations because it could mean the difference between life and death, literally and figuratively. Innocent bystanders can become victims, property damage can add up quickly, and when the police get involved, it is not a good night for anyone. Our bar was a pretty calm environment, for the most part. We developed a staff that was levelheaded and quick to act. If we could deal with an outburst without disrupting the evening's festivities and a large portion of the crowd oblivious to it, it was a job well done. Some of the incidents boil over, and the best thing you can do is try to minimize the collateral damage as best you can.

I've mentioned the local 1 percent motorcycle club that frequented our establishment, and for this story, I will affectionately refer to them as *bikers*. The thing about most bikers is that they are very generous. Charity drives are a huge part of their activities, and they regularly give back to the communities around them. They have regular jobs, or at least most of them do, and they are no different than me or you. It is a group of individuals who share a love for the wind rushing through their hair and the open road before them. There is something freeing about straddling a motorcycle and just riding. There is another side to the lifestyle though. This doesn't pertain to everyone who belongs to motorcycle clubs or look the part, but it is true for the 1 percent club in any given area of the country. When I say the 1 percent, what I mean is the large MCs—you know, the famous ones? You can find documentaries on them, books, articles. They are famous for a reason. Usually, that reason is not a positive one. If you wanted to start your own MC up with a group of friends, you can count on a visit from the 1 percent to check out what you are all about, to ensure that the proper respect is given to the lead dogs. There is a hierarchy, and the 1 percent has several affiliate clubs underneath them who are eyes and ears for the club, of sorts. I'm not completely sure about how someone joins their ranks, but I do know that it involves a period when they are on a probationary trial period, commonly known as a prospect.

It was the summer of 2000 something, and the bar was having a very good year. A new flock of *third shifters* (see the Prologue for descriptions of the shifts) had started coming around. The younger crowd was always filling out with fresh-faced drunkards. Much to the chagrin of the HBIC, we had added a second bartender on Friday nights to help with the growing crowd number. HBIC was older, but she could still sling the drinks with the best of them. She didn't take guff from anyone, she was quick with pours, and she was the longest tenured bartender we had. We had a connection that was built over time, and we could read each other's expressions and body language well. This was important for many reasons, and tonight, it would be put to the test. Because the crowd sizes were getting bigger weekly, I convinced my bosses that I needed to add at least one more person to the staff to man the back door. I was usually pretty good about catching everyone who came through either door to ensure they were legally allowed to be in the bar, but lately, it had become harder. They left it up to me who to hire, and after sifting through a stack of macho mixed martial–art fans rife with testosterone, I found my guys. We now had three members of our security staff on Fridays and Saturdays. I manned the front door, we had a floater/barback, and a person at the back. Those two rotated halfway through the night, and I stayed put at the front door. It was a good system.

Like every other Friday night before this one, it started off normally. At 10:00 p.m., the crowd started growing, and the second-floor guy showed up. At midnight, our third guy arrived. 8-Ball was riling the crowd up with his patented jokes, and surprisingly, the singers for the night weren't awful. Our bar was grandfathered into the liquor laws of the county, which allowed us to stay open longer than the other bars around us. When the other places closed their doors at 2:00 a.m., their patrons would flock to us for the last two hours of the night. Our crowd size would almost double in those short two hours. At 1:00 a.m., I noticed one of the bikers come through the back door. He wasn't one of the regulars like Big Joe or Red, but I recognized his patches and colors. His name was Kong, and he was every bit of a beast like his namesake. A few minutes later, the new bartender brought the phone over to me. One of the other bartenders in town sent chills down my spine when she said, "Hey, Ricky, just wanted to give you a heads-up. It's prospect night, and they just left here."

My head immediately snapped to the back door as a large group of bikers entered the building led by their leader, Sponge. I waved over the barback and told him he needed to man the door. I gave him the phone and told him that he would need to call 911 on my signal. He looked at me confused, and I told him not to worry and that he would know when I gave the signal. It was so cliche and straight out of a movie, but there was no doubt in my mind we were about to have an episode.

I started making my way to the bar to let the HBIC know what was going on, but before I made it halfway to her, she nodded at me and gave me a thumbs up. Confident that she was aware of the situation, I continued through the bar to the back entrance, where our new doorman was diligently carding every one of the bikers, biker's ladies, and prospect who came through unfettered by the mounting eruption before him. It was easy to pick out the prospects from the bikers due to the black lettered T-shirts that labeled them as such, and one of them had a clearly visible shiner forming on his right eye. Kong nodded to me as I passed him, and Sponge smiled when I approached him. We exchanged pleasantries, and he ensured me that they were just here to wind down for the night. The smirk on his face told me he knew that I knew that he knew I knew he wasn't being honest. Hindsight is always twenty-twenty, and I should have tried to get them back through the door and stopped before things went sideways, but I stepped aside and let them enter. I informed my doorman what to look out for, and I noticed in his eyes the same sinking feeling in my stomach. I went to the middle of the room, where I could keep an eye on the crowd and, more importantly, my staff could see me.

The bikers took up residency in my customary football watching seat and ordered some drinks. If you are from the Chicago land area, you may have heard a liquor by the name of Jeppson's Malort, and instinctively, your mouth puckered. Malort served two purposes at our bar. It was a novelty for us, and we made up different shots with it and had a club; if you tried all the shots (not in one night), we would get you a bar T-shirt. The other more practical application of the beverage was for people whom we wanted to leave the bar. It looked enough like whiskey that when it was poured, you couldn't tell the difference. A game had developed called Malort Roulette. The bartender would pour several whiskey shots and one Malort and cover it with a towel. When she pulled it, the group would reach in, grab a glass, and shoot. Immediately, you could tell who the loser was by their facial expressions. Sponge ordered up a Roulette Wheel and had all the prospects participate. They all laughed when the loser had been presented. Sponge leaned up and whispered something in his ear, and the prospect nodded. When Sponge turned from the prospect, he looked me directly in the eyes smiling and shrugged. Time stopped as I watched the prospect slowly move toward a group of new third shifters. It felt like my feet were in cement shoes as I went into action. HBIC, aware of the situation, frantically motioned to 8-Ball to cut the music, but he didn't see the cue. I arrived at the table in time to hear the naive patron ask what prospect wanted. The prospect said, "You're about to find out!" He swung at the unsuspecting drinker. I was able to intercept the first strike by grabbing the assailant's arm in the middle of the swing. The powder keg had been lit.

In an instant, the remaining prospects entered the arena, and the target's friends joined as well. A full-on movie-style brawl erupted. A prospect pushed another person, and the table toppled over, causing a domino effect to happen. People were pushed into one another, and anger turned into violence. In an instant, the number of combatants grew, and I was in the middle of it. I glanced to the front door and yelled for backup, but he was distracted by a young lady and hadn't seen my signal to call the police. Turning my head to the back door, I realized another mistake, Kong. He was in between me and the other doorman. A sudden dread overcame me when the realization I was alone in this hit me. It wasn't the first time that a situation like this had occurred. I launched into action. I was able to get some of the women removed from the situation, leaving the male combatants to their own devices. The crowd squeezed in all around me, yet I remained calm. Thoughts weren't coming. I just reacted. Push a person out of the way here, scoop a girl, and half toss her out of the way. From behind me, I felt a push and turned to deal with what was behind me. My hands went up defensively, and I pushed. Unfortunately for me, I grabbed Kong's girlfriend right in the bosom. Her knee flashed up, and a blast of pain went through my groin. Instinctively, I moved forward to get her out of the fight, and with my stomach in knots, I went back into the fight. Have you ever watched an old cowboy movie where a bar room brawl breaks out? Glass bottles are shattered over heads, chairs are broken over backs, and someone eventually pulls a knife. Well, speaking from experience, I can say that two of those things are untrue. A prospect swung a beer bottle at one of the guys, and I jumped in front of him—hello, concussion number six. The glass didn't break, but it hurt like hell. From the corner of my eye, I witnessed one of the third shifters swing a bar stool at a prospect, connecting squarely in the back, and the chair endured.

It took me longer to write the description of those events than they happened in real time. Eventually, my two staffers were able to help, and within minutes, the bar cleared as lights and sirens filled the parking lot. The bikers never got involved in the physical confrontation and played dumb when the police questioned them. Most of the prospects were arrested and placed in the back seats of squad cars. When I was being questioned, an officer asked if I was all right or needed medical attention. I said I was fine. He pointed to my arm where a steady stream of blood was flowing from the back of my elbow. When I looked at it, I noticed a chunk was missing. No clue how that happened. I climbed into the back of the ambulance to get looked over. While they were looking me over, I felt a little lightheaded. I chalked it up to being mashed in the head with a beer bottle. The EMT said something about blood pooling on the cot and asked me to lift my shirt. Remember the two truths and a lie? Well, the beer bottle and the chair didn't break. I had two small puncture wounds at my back that were no bigger than an inch wide. Blood was flowing out of them, and I realized my pants and shirt were sopping. During the fracas, I just figured beer and alcohol were being spilled on me. They applied pressure and raced me to the ER.

There was no serious damage to anything inside, and they stitched me up. HBIC picked me up and brought me home. Not a word was spoken until we pulled into my driveway. She said, "Nice work. See ya tomorrow."

And I responded, "You know it. Have a good one."

5

I Hit a Guy

When I decided to enter into the bar business as a bouncer, I was like most twenty-somethings who pursue that path: young, invulnerable, and ready to fight at the drop of a hat. At the first place I worked, fights and altercations weren't really a thing. Occasionally, someone would get out of line, and I would have to escort them out of the building, or in the rare instance, like the fight that led to my hire, a brawl would start. My main task was to ensure that we didn't have any underage people inside. However, the second place I worked at was different, altogether. Once or twice a week, the emotions brought on by alcohol, youth, and machismo would roll into a fight or two. Close spaces and crowded places are a perfect set of ingredients for volatile situations. In all the time I worked at the second place, I only threw a punch twice. It was at the same person, two years apart. I would like to think that I am a fair person, especially when it came to working the door. People do things when they are intoxicated that they wouldn't normally do. They're bolder and more talkative, and sometimes, they are just downright jerks. Because alcohol is the usual culprit, I tried my best not to hold grudges or judge someone's behavior. Behind the drunken haze is a person, after all. Some people, however, do not need any help being rude. It is just part of who they are. We had a lot of them come through the doors over the years, but one stands out in my mind more than any other. I'll call him *Talk Show* because his last name was the same as a popular bespectacled white-haired talk show host from the eighties.

Unlike Friday nights, Saturday had a gradual increase in population. Friday nights, the crowd came in waves, while Saturday, there was a steady trickle. The crowd for both days ended the same though—shoulder to shoulder, butt to butt, and wall to wall. Despite the large crowds, Saturdays were easier to manage. Even the late-night rush was easier to deal with simply because they didn't all come at once. There was a sports-themed eatery/pub in town where some of the young attractive women in the area worked as waitstaff, and when they would close, they would venture over to our place to wind down. The young male clientele would follow them mouths agape and tongues wagging. I became friendly with most of the servers, and our bartenders would try their hardest to make sure they were well taken care of. Professional courtesy, of sorts, that would be returned when we would visit them on their turf. Like us, they had a group of regulars. They were comprised of friends of the staff who were similar in age. They all attended the same high school, went to the same colleges, and knew each other for years. My assumption is that most of us have, or are a part of, a group like that. There is always one or two people in those groups that are annoying, rude, and a pain in the ass. We overlook their faults because of familiarity. "That's just the way they are," we tell ourselves and others.

Talk Show belonged to a group like this, and he was their idiot. He was slight in build and had an arrogance you could see from a mile away. One of the first times I carded him, he made it clear that the owner of the bar was personal family friend. I nodded and told him I didn't care who he knew and he needed to show me his identification. I suppose that was all it took for me to get on his list. I can be an ass with the best of them. When the same people go to the bar again and again, you get used to seeing them, and the need to card them becomes less and less. I would make Talk Show show me his ID every time he came in. He would stand nearby and say things to me to see if I would get angry. It never worked. I have dealt with people like him my whole life, and they are just a grain of sand to me. I don't know what he did for work, but whatever it was, he believed that it made him important. He would try to leverage that with the girls he would hit on. It rarely worked, and usually, he just came off as a supercreep. He was obsessed with one of the girls from the sport's pub and would say the rudest things to her. I never heard any of it, but the way she would avoid him made me uncomfortable with him in a bar full of young vulnerable women.

One night, she came in and told me Talk Show was being especially creepy. When he arrived, I carded him, and he just stared at me. He was obviously drunk. It wasn't my call whether he should be served more. That was on the bartenders. When he entered, I got the attention of HBIC and gave her the signal to watch him. She nodded, and the night proceeded. We weren't particularly crowded that evening, so I was able to watch him closer. He went over to his group and stared at the girl of his obsession. She moved to a different table, and seconds later, he got up and followed. This went on for some time, and eventually, she got fed up with it. She stood up, said something to him, and turned to go to the bathroom. He got up immediately and followed. Her path was not directly toward me, but she glanced at me, and when we made eye contact, I saw that she was distraught. I started to wade through the crowd to intercept. When I got near them, I could hear the names he was calling her. There was a line for the women's room, and she took her place. He walked right up next to her, oblivious that I was standing near him. Her face was turning red with anger. He leaned into whisper something, she leaned away, and then he put his hand on her breast and said, "You know you like it."

That was all I needed. She slapped him, and I grabbed him. It wasn't very hard for me to move him; it was like picking up a bag of mulch. He started protesting, and I just guided him to the door. His friends came over and were trying to convince me that he was just being Talk Show. I wasn't afraid of him trying to get physical with me, so I wasn't really paying him much attention. I looked at his friend and said, "He has to go." When I looked back at Talk Show, he spat in my face. There aren't many things that can get me boiling, but spitting on me is one of them. Instinctively, my right fist shot out and connected squarely with his nose. Blood spurted out, and he crumpled. I grabbed him by the shirt and dragged him outside. I dumped him on the ground, went inside, and told his friends, "If he comes back in, it will be worse."

The next day, the owner called me to see what had happened. I told him in great detail how it all went down. He took my side, and Talk Show was banned from coming to the bar. It wasn't all roses for me though. I had committed battery, and as such, I paid those consequences. My boss paid for my legal fees. There was no jail sentence, but I was put on probation, had community service, etc.

For the next two years, the group would come in regularly. Whenever I went to the sport's pub, if she was there, she would give me her family discount. Many times that I was eating there, Talk Show was in the building. He would sit across the bar and stare at me. Sometimes, he would try to come over, but he would be cut off by a member of their staff. The story of what happened was all over town. After a year, his friends would ask every Friday and Saturday if it was okay if Talk Show came back. I would just laugh at them. There were times when Talk Show would try to sneak in the back and hang out in a corner where he thought I couldn't see him. It always ended the same, him scurrying out the back and his friends laughing the whole time. I was not amused. One day, the owner called me and said he had had a conversation with Talk Show. Apparently, he was really sorry and had changed his ways. I was asked what I thought about him being let back in. I told him it was a bad idea but, ultimately, it was the owner's call. I said I would be all right with it, as long as Talk Show apologized to me. The next Saturday, their entire group showed up. Talk Show was at the back of the crowd and last through the door. He handed me his ID, unprompted, and looked me right in the eyes when he said he was sorry. I accepted and shook his hand—no grudges, right?

Unlike the night two years prior, Talk Show seemed in control of his faculties. I admit, I was impressed that he had changed. It is not an easy thing to do, and he seemed like he had become more mature. I didn't hold a grudge, but I didn't forget either. As the night grew later, he consumed more and more alcohol. It wasn't long before I noticed a shift in him. He slumped a little, and the smirk he used to have had slowly found its way back to his face. His eyes became a little glossy, and he started staring at people again. This time, however, it wasn't a girl that was his focus. I didn't stare back at him because I was working, but every time I glanced his way, he was intently looking at me. With a red face, he finally gathered the courage to approach me. The first words out of his mouth were: "You're an asshole," and I nodded and agreed. He then started to lament about his broken nose and how I made him look bad. He was going on and on, and his friends eventually realized what was happening. A crowd started gathering around us, and he was becoming more aggressive with his words. His best friend tried to intervene, but it was too late. Talk Show had entered into a state of drunkenness that leads down the path of irredeemable consequences. I took his beer from his hands and set it on the countertop next to me. I told him he had enough and he could come back tomorrow and settle his tab. I lightly escorted him into the vestibule and toward the exit. When he got to the door, he turned with a huge grin on his face and spit on me again! I reacted in the same fashion, but when I hit him this time, there was a glass door behind him that he fell into. It shattered, and I threw him out of the doorway and onto a car that had just pulled up. His friends filtered out behind us. I stood over him, anger releasing from every pore in my body. He looked up at me and started to move as if he wanted to fight. I pointed at him and told him if he got up, I would break his head. The familiar blue and red lights of the police department rolled into the parking lot. Talk Show was sprawled on the ground, and the crowd had mostly gone back inside. The outcome the second time around was different as well. Instead of me being placed under arrest for battery, they read Talk Show his rights and threw him into the back of the car. Apparently, spitting on someone is also battery. It was still on my face when the cops arrived, and since it went down in the vestibule, there was no footage of me hitting him—lucky break for me, I guess.

Talk Show was banned permanently from our establishment. Well, as long as I worked there, he wasn't allowed in. What his fate was after I left I don't know. I paid for the damages to the door of the bar to avoid insurance claim stuff and all that. When I look back, I find it funny. In eleven years as a bouncer, I have dealt with altercations in the same way, calmly getting the parties separated with as little physical contact as possible. Sure, I would grapple with people from time to time. I have only thrown a punch at a patron twice. Thanks to Talk Show, it was only at one person.

6

I Don't Think That's
Where That Goes

Over the course of a decade, many strange things can happen at a bar. One of the biggest benefits to working in the industry is meeting people from all walks of life. Some of them are good apples, some of them are bad apples, and some of them are pears pretending to be apples. The nature of our pub allowed for a dynamic range of people. I have previously described them using the term *shifts*. I try hard not to be judgmental of people because I don't know what is going on in their lives to cause certain behaviors, but there is a group of people that I do not like. No, I downright hate them. Drug dealers are some of the worst that humanity has to offer this world. I am not talking about the local kid who peddles marijuana. I'm talking about the scum who pushes the hard stuff—crack, cocaine, and meth. Those people are evil. Addiction runs rampant in my family. Alcohol, drugs, work, and other stimuli grab a hold of us, and we just can't help it. We fall into the normal cycles of addictive behavior, and it can be hell trying to right our ships. When I see these predators plying their wares onto someone, it boils me from the inside.

There are many reasons why people go to bars. Escape is a prominent one. Being able to forget your life for a little while, or in some instances permanently, is comforting to those who find the world is often cruel. Witnessing the stages of inebriation caused me to have a softer spot for people. More often than not, alcohol quickly loses its potency, and the people start seeking a stronger remedy. The dealers swoop in and offer a *way out* with promises of friendship and solace. Our resident supplier was no different. We weren't his only haunt, but we were a popular one. I was shocked at the number of people who frequented us that were VIP members of his club. His preferred substance was cocaine, and he supplied it in bunches. He had a network of people whom he used to transport, intercede, and find new clientele. Since most of our patrons were shared with other bars in town and we were always the last spot on their trips, it was easy for him to expand. I watched night after night as people, who I usually had so much respect for, would bow down when he came to the bar. He had a friendly arrangement with the 1 percent MC in town, so he had muscle on his side as well.

I assume that the relationship was purely monetary because the club itself was split on their feelings of him. As long as he greased their palms, he could operate. Although he controlled the supply lines, we had a mutual unspoken understanding. He knew that I had friends that were members of the local police force and would never get caught talking in the bar or dealing inside. Anytime someone would approach him, they would go outside to conduct their business. There was an active operation to take him and his suppliers down, which rivaled any primetime television show. I was approached by law enforcement on a regular basis to help set him up, but I didn't want anything to do with that. I am brave and stupid at times, but I do not have a death wish. Eventually, the lifestyle would catch up to him, and he got caught. For what it's worth, he didn't flip on anyone and took the fall completely.

I watched too many people fall to his trap. It really is a sad thing to witness. I have seen a beautiful young girl mesmerized by his flashy car and big spending, get caught up in his wake, and become a horrible shell of herself. She became his steady girlfriend and stayed by him even when he would cheat repeatedly on her. Addiction is powerful. He would get his friend's significant others hooked, and then when they needed a fix and if they didn't have money, he would demand sexual favors. Prominent businessmen in town, lonely housewives, and anyone else looking for some fun would get stuck in his web. It disgusted me that I couldn't do anything about it. His closest friends tried to be friendly with me, and I was cordial with them, but the disdain was written on my face. Now, he wouldn't deal or talk about it in the bar, but his customers didn't have that level of respect. They would get their stash and enter the bathrooms to use. Groups of girls would go into the bathroom to party, and people could hear them outside. On numerous occasions, our female bartenders would come up to me and say, "Ricky, they're doing it again in the bathroom!" There wasn't anything I could do. Unfortunately, I would just have to sit back and watch it unfold. From the outside, it is easy to say, "Well, just ban him from the bar." It isn't that easy. When a business relies on sales to survive, certain things can be overlooked. His reach was so deep that had we banned him, it could have affected our business. We operated on a "don't ask, don't tell" policy, and business went on as usual.

Out of all the people that he corrupted, and yes, I blame him and his predatory behavior, there was one that affected me the most. It was heartbreaking to watch, and there were many times I tried to intervene. *Joe* was young twenty-something when he started becoming a regular. He found his way to our place by means of one of our softball teams. Joe was smart, shy, and a nice person. He attended one of the local medical schools and had designs on being a pediatrician someday. The world was his oyster. At first, he started only coming on game days and was usually a one-and-done beer drinker. After all, he had responsibilities. I was really impressed with his work ethic and how strict he stayed to his scheduling. Nothing was going to derail his meteoric rise to the top. Our bar had a closed event for the winter holidays, and it was invite only. Employees were allowed to put people on a list to attend the open bar event. Naturally, as captain of the bar softball team, my list was strictly the team. I had asked Joe for two years before he accepted the invitation.

Our staff took turns working the door to make sure that everyone had their invitations. It was a big deal in town to be invited to our holiday party, a night only rivaled by the Wednesday before Thanksgiving. I was working the door when the dealer and his girl came through. This was my opportunity to shut him out. The smile on his face when he handed me his invitation was infuriating. How was this possible? Who gave him the invite? I checked the written list, to make sure that one of his clients didn't just give him theirs, and his name was on the second page. I immediately knew who invited him and her tenure at our bar wouldn't last much after that. That was the end of my celebration. I put my bouncer hat on, and my eyes didn't leave the dealer while he was in the bar for the rest of the night. The dealer approached the table with the softball guys, his beautiful arm candy in tow, and Joe was enamored with her. He could not stop staring at her. The dealer saw this and encouraged her to flirt with him. I was able to catch Joe when they went to conduct business elsewhere. I emphatically warned him about the situation, and he assured me that there was nothing to be worried about. He didn't leave their side the rest of the night.

The next week, Joe showed up on a Wednesday night and then on Friday night. It wasn't long until he was coming in with the late crowd on a regular basis, usually in the company of the dealer. A few different times, I tried to talk to him about the people he was hanging out with, and once, I almost told him about the active investigation to deter him. He told me there was nothing to worry about and laughed it off. The next few months, I watched him spiral into chaos. He was at the bar almost as much as I was, and it wasn't too long before he flunked out of school. He stopped playing softball with us, he got fired from his part-time job, and he moved out of his parents' house. Drugs screw with a person in so many ways. Addiction is a powerful enemy. Physically, the toll his usage took was unmistakable. In only a few months, he lost half his body weight, his eyes became sunk into his head, and he was extremely irritable. I realized that he wasn't just hooked on cocaine at that point. He became the dealer's lackey. Anything the dealer would ask for he would do, no questions asked. Joe moved into the dealer's home. As long as he did his master's bidding, he was paid. His income? Yep, drugs. Like most of his victims, the dealer quickly got tired of Joe when he became a liability. He kicked him out of the house, cut him off from his supply, and relegated him back to regular junkie status.

I had a soft spot for Joe because I felt partly responsible. I don't now, but I did then. The influence that the dealer had at the other establishments in the area got Joe banned from most of them, but we let him continue to come to us. He always had money for drinks, and he didn't bother anyone, so he was harmless. Most of the money he had, and I am not sure how he came about it, went up his nose. The dealer would show up, and Joe would go outside with him to talk.

One night, Joe was a little more animated than usual. He sat at the bar and didn't order any drinks, just water. When the dealer arrived, he went to talk to him, and the dealer laughed at him. They were close enough to me that I could hear Joe say that he didn't have any money but he was good for it. Anger flashed across the dealer's face, and he caught my eye. He grabbed Joe by the arm and dragged him out the back door. I was concerned, so I followed them outside. They had a hushed conversation, and all I could make out was the dealer saying that Joe knew what he had to do. They went back inside, with the dealer patting me on the shoulder as he passed. Inside, Joe returned to his seat, shifting uncomfortably every couple of minutes. About a half hour later, Joe got up and approached the dealer, and they headed toward the back door. We had just started getting busy so I couldn't follow. Ten minutes later, a girl approached me and said that they saw two guys go into the women's room. She described Joe and used the dealer's first name. This couldn't be good. I flagged one of the other guys to man the door so I could go deal with this. A line had started to form at the bathroom, and I waded through a sea of females to the door. I banged on it once and yelled that they needed to get out of there. It was very loud inside the bar that night, and I couldn't hear a response. I banged again and got the previous response. I put my ear to the door and heard muffled grunts. Thoughts raced through my head. *Were they fighting? Were they engaging in some lewd activity?* Regardless of what I thought was going on, this needed to be resolved.

I reared back and kicked the door. I have seen it done in movies before, so I was pretty much an expert. The flimsy door caved to my powerful kick, and the doorjamb splintered. The door swung violently open, and the sight I saw was extremely disturbing. They weren't fighting. There was no oral sex going on. Joe had his hands on the sink counter. His pants were around his ankles, and the dealer was standing behind him. I know what you're thinking. They were engaging in butt sex. You would be right. However, you wouldn't be completely right. The dealer was positioned behind Joe, fully clothed. In his hands was the toilet plunger. He was shoving the handle of the plunger into the rear end of a groaning Joe. There was an audible gasp of shock from behind me from a gaggle of women waiting to use the facilities. The only thing I could think of to say was, "Um…I don't think you are using that correctly."

The dealer was kicked out of the bar for a week, and Joe never showed his face around the area again. The incident was the talk of the town, and jokes were made daily. I could never look at the dealer in the eyes again. It was a funny incident, to say the least, but there was a deep and profound sadness to it all.

In a year's time, I watched Joe go from a promising young doctor to a drug addict. Addiction is powerful and will cause you to do things that aren't normal.

A year after I left the business for good, Joe's mother got in touch with me. As soon as she said who she was, I knew what she was about to tell me. Joe lost his battle to addiction. He had fallen so far off his track that he couldn't find his way back. He took his own life to escape his demons. I will always feel partly responsible for his outcome, but I know that there was nothing I could have done differently. It wasn't until I watched my sister tirelessly work to beat her addiction that the power of addiction was fully realized. There are many things that I have seen in the bar, but this was by far the saddest.

# 7

She Knocked Him Out

Every bar has legends. Some are feats of wonder; others are people. However, some of them are both. On certain rare occasions, a person will enter a pub and do something that stands the test of time. These stories are passed from patron to patron and take on lives of their own. They are shaped by the awe in which they are told and morph into legendary myths akin to that of the famous *Iliad*. Often met with disbelief, the tale is corroborated by eyewitness accounts and hearsay from reliable bystanders. The participants in these yarns are usually timid or shy about them, which lends to the wonderment of the story itself. If the act is witnessed by a crowd, it becomes more than something that happened; it becomes integral to the identity of the establishment. It's as if people witnessed a great moment in history and is talked about for years after. One time at the bar, I witnessed the birth of one such legend, and this is the tale.

The holiday season was approaching quickly, and with it, crowd sizes increased. I had established myself as a figurehead at the bar. There were a few people whom I didn't know or recognize, but I knew most of the patrons' names. Occasionally, new members to the ranks would appear, and it wouldn't be too long before I added them to my memory bank. One thing that helped me in my work was my ability to remember faces and names. It is a blessing and a curse. This particular night, the bar was full of people that I knew. Tensions were high because of the season, and people were more on edge than they normally would be. It happened every year at the same time. Pressures from family functions, work, and gift buying would build up over time, and people would look for an outlet. Altercations between people increased, and the number of people we would have to escort out of the building doubled. Relationships would get strained, and people would act out. One positive from the time of the year was I would get to see people who didn't come in on a regular basis.

One couple who only came three or four times a year started popping in on a weekly basis. They were the parents of one of our younger regulars and were an absolute delight to talk with. They would spend time talking with other bar goers but would always make it over to talk with me for most of the evening. Conversation would undoubtedly turn to their daughter, and they thanked me for watching out for her. It was an easy task to do. Their daughter was a fun person and always respectful and made everyone smile. She was an extremely tiny girl, but her personality was huge. She was the center of attention, and everyone lit up when she came to the bar. She inherited that from her parents. All the customers knew their names, bought them drinks, and became happier in their presence. Tensions would deflate while they were at the bar, and the staff appreciated this beyond measure.

We added a fourth person to the staff during the holiday season to help with crowd sizes and the increased consumption of alcohol. This changed the layout of what post I would assign people. I became the floater and would walk the floor to keep a solid eye on the crowd. We had a person manning the front and back doors and one barback. From the center of the room, I could easily see the entire bar, and the entirety of the bar could see me. It was a happy crowd this night, and the mood was jovial, until the dealer came in. He was accompanied by his lackeys, and you could feel the happiness get sucked out of the room when people realized he was there. He had this constant smirk that made you want to punch him in the face. The mood gradually shifted to anxiousness merely due to his existence. The festive season not only brought people to the bar for a reprieve, but it also increased his business. He didn't have a steady girlfriend at this moment and had been seen around with various girls. Immediately, the parents approached me and asked me about him. Without divulging too much information about him, I said I wasn't a fan and that he caused a lot of issues. That was when I found out their daughter had been *seeing* him over the last month or two. They were rarely in the bar together, and if they were, you would never know that they knew each other. I was completely shocked. She, nor her friends, had mentioned anything about it once. Besides that, and I am no expert, she didn't appear to have been caught in his web of drugs and deception. All in all, it seemed she found out about him quickly and ended it. That made me happy.

For the rest of the night, I kept an eye on that situation. The father seemed to care little of the dealer and paid him hardly any attention. However, the mother was staring daggers at him. You know the saying if looks could kill? Well, if that were true, he would have been dead ten times over. The daughter didn't seem to be affected by his presence either. The dealer was minding his business, and that settled me to a certain extent. When the dealer went into the billiards room, the mother and father changed their position as well. I watched as she tapped her husband on the arm and moved to a spot adjacent to the pool tables. They had been drinking a little more than usual. I felt the anger pouring out of her, and I moved my post accordingly. I placed myself between them to intercept any altercation. It didn't take long for the dealer to see me or the mother staring at him. I think the daughter had sensed something, and she came up behind her mom and dad. The dealer began smiling and walked over to talk to me. He never took his eyes of the mother. I started to say something when she interjected. She asked the dealer what he was looking at, and he responded that she looked familiar. The dad placed his beer on the counter and turned in a menacing stance. Swear words started coming out of the mom at a rate that would make a truck driver blush. The father's hands balled up into fists, and the dealer just stood there smiling. The daughter tried to calm her mother down, but it was futile. The dealer just took it, all while grinning and chuckling. When she finished her verbal bashing, the dealer laughed and gestured to her daughter. Then he said, "She didn't mind me while I was pulling those cute pigtails from behind," and mimicked the act in front of her parents. Instantly, the dad's face turned blood red with anger, and the mother's jaw dropped to the floor. Before I could even move from behind the father, a tiny object leaped into the air. Time crawled to a stop as I watched the form of this small human girl jump into the air, arm cocked. I swear I looked back and forth between her and the dealer at least ten times while she was airborne. I froze. After what seemed like an hour, her fist connected on the sweet spot of the jaw. His eyes rolled back into his head, and he started to fall backward. I started to move toward him, but it felt like I was moving through mud. I watched helplessly while he fell toward the pool table behind him. I feared that he would smack his head on his way down. That would be the end of everything. He was going to die, we were going to get shut down, and there was nothing I could do about it. Luckily, he missed the table. Time returned to normal, and all hell broke loose. His entourage dashed to his aid, the mother and father corralled their rabid animal, and I stood in the doorway, blocking the two groups from one another.

We were able to calm everyone down quickly. Much to my dismay, I had to have a conversation with the daughter and her parents. We had a rule at our bar regarding physical altercations. Any kind of physical violence would be an automatic ban. It was permanent in most cases, but we would make exceptions for people who were regulars. I had to escort her from the building, and her parents were pleading for forgiveness. They kept asking me if I had heard what he had said and why I wasn't kicking him out. It is never easy to explain this situation to people. It is even harder to explain it to people whom I respected. The truth of it all is that words don't matter at all in these situations. He said what he said, and she punched him. My hands were tied, and I had to do my job. I never play favorites in these situations. As much as I hated the dealer, the right thing to do was kick her out. I didn't need to discuss this with bartenders or the ownership; it was my decision. I told her she had a week timeout, and she told me to go have intercourse with myself. I was a little sad, but I knew that she was still angry. I said I was sorry and that she could come back in a week. All three of them had choice words for me as they left.

Reluctantly, I went into the bar and approached the dealer. When these fights break out, protocol dictates that we ask the victim if they would like us to call the police. I knew he would say no, but I also knew that he was not going to let this go. I pulled him aside and told him that he needed to not pursue this on his own. He laughed at me and asked what I would do about it. I looked him dead in the eyes and told him that if anything happened to any of those three, I would come looking for him. He knew that I knew people too. He also knew that I had a fantastic relationship with the 1 percent, even though he had a working one with them and mine was more of a brotherhood. They would have my back unequivocally.

For the next week, the story grew. We had a regular David and Goliath on our hands, and it snowballed. It was said that she leaped ten feet through a crowd to reach him. Some instances of the story told how she vaulted over me or even that I caught her but her tenacity was too much for me to handle. I didn't bother correcting them. It was fun to hear the variations. People who saw it asked me why I didn't stop it. They assumed that because it was the dealer, I just let it happen. I didn't correct that narrative either. I never told anyone that I just froze. I think that part of me let it happen because I wanted him to be punched in the face—that stupid smirk. It really didn't matter. The reach of the story went to other bars, and our first and second shifters would ask me to tell them. Most of them relished the idea of the dealer getting whacked. I obliged every time. On the day her suspension was lifted, we had an inordinate amount of holdover from the previous shifts. She, and her parents, entered the building at around ten o'clock to a resounding cheer. Her face flushed with embarrassment, and she tried to make herself smaller than she already was. They made their way through the crowd, amid pats on the backs and hugs, toward me. All three of them apologized to me for the things that they said, and we hugged it out. They explained that they understood the situation I had been put in and respected the fact that I did my job without espousing favoritism. That made me smile. For the rest of the night, they drank for free. It felt like everyone in the bar was buying for them. About an hour after their arrival, I was manning the front door, and the dealer entered the building. It was like a scene from a movie. The crowd went silent, and from the karaoke stage, 8-Ball said, "Oh boy." I stood in front of him, blocking his entrance. I shook my head and told him that he wasn't allowed in tonight. His groupies started to protest, but he held his hand up and nodded. They turned around and left. When I turned back to face the room, another cacophony of cheers rumbled across the room. As long as I worked at the bar from that point, our *David* never spent a dime buying her own drinks again.

8

I Saved His Life

Becoming familiar with the people who were regulars at the bar was a point of pride for me. Being able to establish relationships with the patrons makes for a better experience, in my opinion. I was friendly with everyone, and not so much when I needed to be. The different *shifts* allowed me to experience a wide breadth of personalities, ages, and cliques of the clientele. Adding alcohol to the different situations allows for some interesting, and at times scary, scenarios. I have spent many nights in sidesplitting laughter because people's inhibitions seem to take a back seat to the provocation of the spirits. Not all interactions are positive. The reasons people go to the bar vary as much as the shape of a snowflake. Some people are looking for an escape from their boring lives. Men and women alike search for that "something" that makes them feel whole. It has always been a point of wonder for me. Infidelity, in general, is not something that I am fond of. There was an ad campaign that stated, "What happens in Vegas stays in Vegas," but that rule seems to be a universal truth among bar goers.

Through my different responsibilities at the bar, I became friends with a young man. I'll call him Junior, whom I would normally not enjoy sharing space with. Everything about him would, in an outside work situation, annoy me greatly. However, I had to show some modicum of friendship while working. He was one of the people I dubbed a *swing shifter*. He would come in during the second grouping, around 8:00 p.m. and stay well into the night, often closing the bar down. On most days before my shift, I would eat dinner at the bar. We had a Mexican grill that rented our kitchen space for a small rental fee, and their food was delicious. Junior would join me most nights, and it was through that shared space that I started to grow a little fond of him. He became a pseudo-little brother to me. You know how when you have younger siblings everything they do is overtly annoying, but you can't help but smile at them because of their dumb antics? That was Junior. Some of the things he would say would make me shake my head in disbelief. All in all, he was a pretty good kid. We all make mistakes when we are younger, and he was no different.

Junior had a penchant for the ladies. He wasn't a horrible-looking kid, and I suppose his sophomoric ruses could be endearing to some. Like most young men, he pursued female companionship. Because he spent so much time at our bar, he would go to others in the area, but he would affectionately refer to our place as *his*, and it wasn't long before the womanly clientele got to know him. Some thought he was merely a pest, and others thought he was cute. There is an adage that goes, "Don't eat where you shit," and that is true in most situations. In the bar business, however, there is no shortage of people who eat in the bathroom. Romantic, or physical in the least, relationships figure prominently in the industry. It is an interesting thing to observe from an unhindered seat on the outside. The game of cat and mouse between the opposite sexes can be entertaining. Just the same, it can be devastating to watch. Junior was never deterred from his goal. By today's standards, he might be considered overbearing, but there was no harm in what he was doing, and if a girl was uncomfortable, he would stop and move on. There was little in the way of fear that Junior possessed, and that was a blessing and, much later, a curse. He would harmlessly flirt with women until they reciprocated or shunned him, and he considered anyone in the bar fair game. Whether they were in a relationship, marriage included, didn't bother him. That led to some awkward situations, where I would need to step in if a significant other would get frazzled by his attempts. When that happened, I would pull Junior aside and tell him that one of these times I wouldn't be around to have his back. He would pat me on the shoulder and laugh. We both knew that wasn't true.

Eventually, he would turn his attention to one of the married regulars; we'll call her Rebecca. Rebecca was part of a trio of women in their thirties who frequented the bar. Of her group, she was the only one who was married, and her husband was also a regular. Once or twice a month, they would come to unwind. Her husband and his best friend Big Carl would join them toward the end of the evening. When Junior first crossed paths with the trio, his target was not Rebecca. He initially set his sights on the serial single of the group. She never had a steady boyfriend, or relationship for that matter, and she would flirt with a lot of the guys in the bar. Their *romance* was short-lived and flamed out faster than it started. He started his attempt with Rebecca, and it was almost comical. Watching from my perch, it made me chuckle whenever he would attempt a line and she would, not so kindly, shoot him down. It is my belief that he did it just because she was so mean and it made people laugh around him.

The dynamic changed after about three months of this. She started coming about once a week instead of their regular once-a-month rendezvous. The flirting between them became less frequent but more intense. It was harmless, for the most part, and provided me with something to watch when the crowd wasn't so big. My observations of them would reveal something that should be obvious by now. Their relationship had progressed beyond the *innocent* flirting that we all watched and had crossed over into some turbulent waters. I tried to have a conversation with him about it. He adamantly denied it and said he knew better than to mess with a married woman. After hours, it was brought up, and the HBIC was certain that nothing was going on because she knew Rebecca very well. I was not so sure. Rebecca and Junior were trying hard not to blow their cover, but the little things they did weren't missed by me. After all, my job was to observe and predict things going on in the bar. When he would talk, not flirt, with another girl, she would get upset. Then he would try to smooth it over. In hindsight, I don't believe that none of the other employees missed these clues.

I tried to talk to Junior again. He didn't want to hear it and continued to deny. My thoughts were validated when the trio came out for their monthly gathering, and I overheard the other two talking about it. Their non-relationship continued for a while, and anytime the husband and Big Carl showed up, I would get nervous. If he found out, it wasn't going to be a fun night. There is a moral quandary that I would deal with many times: do I tell the people involved, or do I hope that it will figure it out? My main goal was to ensure the safety of the people in the establishment. I didn't see the value in telling her husband and hoped that this fire would run out of oxygen first.

While eating dinner one night, my worst fears would be realized. Junior joined me, as usual, and it was slightly more crowded for the time. We ordered our food, had our conversation, and enjoyed the sports game that was on the television. Junior got up to use the washroom. As was the custom, people who sat next to me felt comfortable leaving their things on the bar, knowing that I would keep an eye on them. Junior left his phone when he left. While he was gone, his phone buzzed. There were a couple of guys sitting on the other side of Junior, and they thought it would be funny to mess with his phone. Unfortunately, he didn't lock it behind a password, and this was eons before facial recognition or fingerprinting. While they were trying to change settings or some such, they came across his photos. When I saw the look on their faces, I became concerned. They called the bartender over, and before they could show her what was on the phone, I grabbed it from them. The damage had been done. I looked down at the phone and saw the photos of him and Rebecca in compromising positions. It was a complete invasion of privacy, but I couldn't help myself. I scrolled, quickly, through photo after photo of their illicit affair. I put the phone down on the bar and waited for Junior to return. When he did, the guys sitting next to him started laughing. They moved positions when I glared at them. Junior was confused and was getting mad at the fact that people were laughing at him. I crossed my arms, stared at the TV, and leaned over to him. I said that he really needs to remember to lock his phone if he was going to leave it behind. Instantly, he knew what the issue was. His countenance became as white as a ghost, and he repeated the word *no* over and over.

As the night grew on, he became more nervous. Rumors spread like wildfire, and when you add alcohol to the mix, it becomes out of control. That night, after closing, the employees had a long conversation about it. I warned them that when her husband finds out, it would be hard to control it. I had informed Junior that if he was ever in the bar when her husband showed up that he was to leave immediately, no questions asked, and the staff agreed with me. The only thing we could do now was wait for the explosion. I don't know how we went as long as we did without a confrontation. Her husband found out almost immediately, and Junior heeded my advice about leaving. I had to have a tough conversation with both Rebecca and her husband about it. I told them that I was going to be neutral in the situation and that if anything happened, I would dole out punishment to the one who initiated the issue first. If they couldn't exist in the bar together, they weren't allowed to be in the bar at all. Her husband hated me. I didn't blame him at all for it. Years later, I would feel his pain intimately. Rebecca hated me, and I didn't care at all. Junior didn't hate me, but every time I saw him, he would say how sorry he was and that he should have listened. I didn't gloat; I just worked.

There was one thing I didn't count on, the friendship between her husband and Big Carl. It was a serious misstep on my part. Now, when I say Big Carl, I don't mean in the ironic sense. *He* was a mountain of a man—6'8", 400 pounds, and a former wrestler in the NCAA at Oklahoma University.

When he stood behind, you could feel it. Normally, his demeanor was peaceful, but I was always worried what would happen if he decided he didn't want to play nice. It happened one night when we were severely short-staffed. I was pulling triple duty, watching both doors, bar-backing, and trying to keep an eye on an ever-growing crowd. Junior was there and was up to his old antics. Rebecca and the Trio hadn't been in, in a while, and the word on the street was that she and her husband were trying to work through their problems.

When Big Carl came through the back door, I didn't think much about it. However, when I saw him ask someone a question and the person pointed to the bar in the direction that Junior was sitting, my stomach sank. I intercepted Big Carl and tried to make small talk. He had an unsettling smile on his face and patted me on the shoulder. He told me I was good people, and he reeked of booze. He pushed past me and made his way to the bar, directly behind Junior. Without looking at the bartender, he ordered a drink. Junior could feel the shadow and turned to look who was standing over him. I give the credit for holding it together when he saw Big Carl. He stood up and tried to maneuver around Big Carl, but it proved to be a difficult task. Big Carl just stared at him with the smile and didn't move at all. Junior was able to squeeze past him, and Big Carl just stared at him as he walked away. A large crowd of people came through the front door, and I had to go check them. I tried to keep an eye on the Junior and Big Carl situation while checking IDs. Junior made his way to the bathroom line, and Big Carl followed. It was like he was stalking his prey. I watched it all unfold in slow motion. Junior was standing against the wall, and Big Carl took up a spot directly across from him. Big Carl sipped on his beer, the whole time smiling at Junior.

I decided to abandon my post. I waded through the crowd toward the bathroom. Junior said something to Big Carl, and the smile disappeared from his face. He reached up and grabbed Junior around the neck with one hand and lifted him off the ground. Junior's glass crashed to the floor, and both his arms wrapped around Big Carl's forearm. It may seem like an exaggeration, but Junior's feet were two feet off the ground. The color was draining from his face quickly, and his feet were swinging wildly. When I reached them, I jumped into the air and through my body across Big Carl's arm. It worked, and he let go. I could hear Junior gasping for breath. I placed myself in between them and leaned toward Junior and told him not to move, no matter what.

I turned my attention fully toward Big Carl, and I could feel myself getting sick. I'm not a small person, but he dwarfed me. He repeatedly told me to get out of his way. I stared him back in the eyes and said no. I told him it wasn't going to go down the way he thought. He called me names, threatened me, and continued to tell me to get out of the way. I could feel my legs quiver as I stared him back and stood my ground. It was the first time in my career that I was truly scared. If it was going to come to blows, this might be where I die. I told Big Carl he had to leave. He laughed and asked who was going to make him. I reminded him that the owners would have my back and if they had to get involved, he wouldn't be welcomed back, ever. Reluctantly, Big Carl turned and left, not before he called me an asshole.

Junior thanked me profusely for saving his life, and slowly, the feeling came back to my body. I told Junior to be quiet, finish his beer, and leave. The crowd was impressed with how I stood up to Big Carl, but I didn't feel like I accomplished anything. I felt like Junior maybe deserved to have his butt kicked a little bit. HBIC said she had never seen Big Carl back down like that before. All these people were saying that I had balls of steel. I couldn't express to them how scared I was or how much I was actually on the husband's side. My relationship with Junior went downhill after that. I never let him forget that I saved his life. When Big Carl would come in, he wouldn't even acknowledge my existence. We would have more incidents in the future, but I had hoped that he respected me for what I had done. I was wrong. You can't win them all, I guess.

9

Frank Smiled

The holiday season can be a tough time for people. The added pressure of family visits, working for the end of year bonus, or just melancholy feelings that accompany the time of year lead some folks to increase the frequency of their bar visits. Our establishment was no different. Shortly after Halloween, the crowd size would gradually increase. One or two people a night more, compounded weekly, and before you knew it, I was adding a door guy to the schedule for every night of the week. Most nights, that was me. There are holidays that people associate with going to taverns. St. Patrick's Day and New Year's Eve are two dates that people, who aren't in the know, believe as the busiest days a bar could have. If you don't know the business, I could see how that could be a choice. Truthfully, the day before Thanksgiving is worse than any other holiday you could possibly think of. It has been dubbed affectionately as Black

Wednesday by those employed in the vocation. We would be at standing room-only capacity by 7:00 p.m., and all the shifts were present and accounted for. Our staff would carry two bartenders, two barbacks, and six *security* members for the night. The name of the night was directly related to Black Friday—you know, the day when people line up for hours outside their favorite stores to get the best possible deal and then stampede the doors when they open? That was the ambiance of Black Wednesday too.

By 10:00 p.m., it would be standing room only. The security staff would be assigned sections to watch. The primary job was to clean up spills and usher people along when they stood for too long in a traffic area. As far as fights and altercations would go, they were few and far between because there was no room. My post on this night never changed. I would watch the entire bar from my normal football-watching position. It afforded me the greatest access to help in various areas. If the bartenders and barbacks got overwhelmed, I could jump in and assist, and if the door became too crowded, I could help there as well.

One particular Black Wednesday, I met a new patron. His name was Frank, and he was an old curmudgeonly fellow. Life had not been easy for this guy, or at least that was the vibe I was getting from him. He came earlier than the crowd, arriving at 6:00 p.m. or so, and from the moment he arrived, we knew that he wasn't going to last the night. He just exuded a general unpleasantness about him. This was his first time in our bar, and as the night grew longer, I thought that maybe it would be his only night. When he ordered his drink, he made a sarcastic remark to the tender when she said she needed help making an old-fashioned. I didn't hear what was said, but it clearly affected her. Before she could wave me over, I approached and asked what the issue was. He looked me up and down but didn't say anything. She asked me if I could help her make an old-fashioned, and as I made my way around to show her, Frank said, "Never mind. I'll have an old style," in a voice that sounded like he smoked four packs of cigarettes for most of his life.

Because the crowd hadn't started gathering yet, I sat down next to him and tried to make small talk. I introduced myself and asked him his name. He gave it begrudgingly and answered the rest of my queries in yes or no fashion. I didn't push the incident too hard; I was just trying to buffer his crankiness. The crowd eventually filled out, and my attentions were drawn elsewhere. I almost forgot that Frank was there, until he wobbled past me and out the door. During the end of the night, meeting Frank was a favorite topic of the bartenders. He made an impression on the staff, and not in the good way. In the three hours he was there, he only consumed three beers, but when he left, it looked like he was hammered. When he arrived, there were no signs that he was inebriated. I chalked it up to an unusually low tolerance, or something else, and didn't pay it any mind. I hoped that he didn't drive home and was told by the door guy that Frank got into a cab when he left. That made me feel better.

Thanksgiving night at the bar is dead. A few stragglers come in after family dinners but nowhere near the crowd for a normal Thursday night. I was working the bar and had one customer when Frank arrived the night after his first appearance. I said hello, and he grunted back. I asked him if he wanted an old-fashioned or an old style. He muttered something under his breath and then asked for a beer. I poured it for him and then went back to my duties. Football was on the television, and after a couple of drinks, Frank started talking about the game. Progress had been made! The small talk for the rest of the night didn't amount to much, but I did get the feeling that he was warming up. Over the course of the next month, Frank became a regular. When I look back, there wasn't a night that he didn't come in from Black Wednesday to Christmas night. Of course, his pleasant demeanor made him a hit with all the bartenders, something I would like to tell you. All the bartenders refused to serve him, except one. The HBIC didn't care much who you were and gave as good as she got. Frank seemed to enjoy that about her. On nights when she or I tended the bar, he would stay until closing, when we would place him in a cab. Other nights, he would be lucky to get two beers from the staff.

I learned a lot about Frank over the next month. His life wasn't the easiest, and he hadn't been in contact with his children for over forty years. His was a tale that is so common among bar regulars—struggles personally or professionally or otherwise leads people by the hand straight to the bottom of a bottle. We can judge from the outside, but that doesn't help the matter at all. One of my favorite things about working at the bar was being able to listen to people's troubles. Sometimes, all you need is an ear. Who better than strangers to tell your troubles too? When Frank would realize when he was opening up too much, he would flip the switch to become a jerk again. That was when we would cut him off and put him in the cab to go home.

Every day for the next month, he would come in, and every day, we would go through our checklist—grumpy Frank, a couple beers; loose Frank, a couple beers; and asshole Frank. Thanksgiving season gave way to Christmas season, and the people would start coming back into the pub. Christmas night, unlike Thanksgiving night, had a decent crowd. Frank rolled in at his favorite time. It was different with him this time. When he arrived, he had the biggest smile! He was happy for once. He said hello and Merry Christmas to everyone he crossed paths with. He wasn't drunk, but he was extremely happy. Another out-of-character move came when he bought a round for those sitting around him. His happiness even led to a decent tip for the bartender, to the shock of everyone. Remember, everyone gets a nickname, and he had been dubbed Dollar Bill. No matter how much he had to drink, he always left one dollar bill as a tip. This time, he left a twenty. I was curious about the change in him. I took a couple of minutes to talk to him. He told me that for the first time in forty years, he had talked to his son that morning. He had an opportunity to apologize to him, and they agreed to meet. He was finally going to meet his grandchildren. My happiness was only overshadowed by his.

Christmas miracles do happen! Even when he got past his normal point of drinking, he stayed jovial. It was such a delight to witness this joy emanating from someone as scrooge-like as him. The Grinch's heart grew ten sizes that say, if you will. The night came to an end, and I put Frank into a cab. He thanked me for being a good person and even hugged me. It's amazing how a little patience works sometimes. I instructed the cabbie to take care of him and then paid the fare myself. I said goodbye to Frank and said I would see him tomorrow. I also reminded him that my birthday was in three days and that he needed to be there to celebrate with me. He laughed and said he couldn't wait.

I didn't think much of the fact that it had been a couple of days that we last saw Frank, until a man came in asking about him. He didn't seem happy at all. His first appearance at the bar was two days after Christmas during the day. When I arrived, Princess told me some guy was in here asking about a man named Frank. Since she was the only bartender who never crossed paths with Frank, she told the man to come back at 6:00 p.m. to talk to me about him. One half hour later, a burly middle-aged man came in the door precisely at 6:00 p.m. I didn't recognize him at all and assumed this was the person asking after Frank. I stuck my hand out in a gesture of good faith and introduced myself. He looked down at my hand and then back up at my face. His first question caught me a little off guard. He asked me if I was the person who thought it was a good idea to serve a recovering alcoholic. I didn't respond immediately, and that was the opening he needed to berate me. I calmly listened, but with every passing name call, I grew more and more agitated. When he was finished, I told him the story of Frank as I knew it. Of course, I had my suspicions that Frank was an alcoholic, but it wasn't my, or anyone in the bar's, responsibility. That angered him even more. I apologized and told him that the last time I saw Frank was Christmas night. I explained the entirety of the night to him. Turns out Frank had been missing for the last two days. This person looking for Frank never gave a name and refused when I asked him who he was. He said he was going to sit at the bar and wait for the bartenders to come to ask questions. I politely told him that he could stay but if he harassed the bartenders or patrons, he wouldn't be welcome here. He laughed and smirked as if to say, "What are you going to do about it?" The time from my conversation with him to kicking him out of the bar was less than three minutes. After he left and after I calmed down, I started thinking about the last night I saw Frank. Did he mention that he was going out of town? Was it to go see his son and grandkids? Was that guy his son? It bothered me the entire night.

My birthday came and went, and Frank still hadn't shown up. The man looking for him showed up the next two days harassing the staff and patrons, and when I showed up, he would leave. On the day before New Year's Eve, a news report came out about a local man who had frozen to death. It was Frank. The snowfall had been great that week. When he got home from his night out, he slipped on his front porch and fell off into a snowbank, breaking his hip in the process. Where he fell was hidden from the view of the neighbors, and the snow was soft enough that he was covered by the fluffy snow when he fell into it. No one knew where to look, and the ensuing snowfall over the days after Christmas covered any signs of his whereabouts. It started warming up on my birthday. Over the next few days, the snow melted enough for Frank to be found. The man who was looking for Frank came to the bar and demanded that we be held responsible. The police got involved, and instead of mourning the loss of a patron, we had to defend ourselves from lawsuits. We were successfully able to show that we weren't liable in any way, but the damage had been done. None of the staff was permitted to attend Frank's memorial service, although I suspect there would have been only a few of us who went regardless.

I was very sad for the loss of Frank. The man who had been looking for Frank turned out to be his brother, and at the court hearings, I was able to meet his son. Against the warning of counsel, I approached him and gave my sincerest apologies. I told his son that he talked about him a lot and was so happy on Christmas that he was finally able to contact him. His son didn't say anything to me, and I wasn't surprised. A few months later, his son walked into our bar. He thanked me for my kind words and assured me that he didn't hold us responsible for his father's death. We talked about Frank and the good days. There were a few that he remembered, but the bad seemed to be more abundant. I called the bartender over and ordered two old-fashioned. We cheered to Frank and mending bridges. I was happy that I got to see Frank smile once before he left.

10

It All Changed

When I first started as a bouncer, I was twenty-one years old. I was at the peak of my physical condition. Also, I had this unwavering thought that I was above harm. Invincibility, or delusions of it, comes standard with most young male packages, or at least they did when I was that age. It wasn't that I thought that I could take on the world or that I was tougher than others, but I had been through some things that should have severely injured, possibly killed, me, and I came out of them with barely a scratch. In my mind, I was given a superpower of sorts. What I should have realized was that I was just a little dumb when it came to physical confrontations. I am not trying to brag about my martial prowess; I am merely giving a glimpse into how I operate in situations. Violence should never be the answer, and I usually can get out of most situations without physicality. However, there are circumstances that require a slightly rougher response, and even though I disdain violent activity, I tend to excel at them. I have an extremely high tolerance for pain during altercations because I am completely unaware of it. This mode activates, and adrenaline takes over, allowing me to shrug off things that happen. At the first bar I worked at, there was a fight that broke out in the area of the washroom, and to get there swiftly, I had to vault a half-wall and press through the crowd. When I landed, I rolled my ankle and fractured it. An hour after the fight had ended, I noticed a throbbing in my ankle. There were other examples earlier in these stories, and I have more from my childhood that show my ability to ignore pain. It was just something that was. It gave me a false sense of security that allowed me to react, instead of thinking before jumping in. I have always been a protector, and for the next ten years, I took it upon myself to ensure that on a nightly basis, the people who frequented our establishment would be safe. There are so many things that could go wrong on any given night in the bar industry. Adding alcohol to the ingredients of the night's activities can result in different results. Some of them can be funny, and some of them can be tragic. How you react to those situations can either put out a fire or it could add fuel and make it go out of control. During the first ten years of my life as a bouncer, I felt completely under control of any situation. On a rare Saturday night off, at a different bar, it all changed.

It took a long time for me to get confident with the security staff before I felt comfortable with not being there on Friday or Saturday night. I had finally found a group of guys who were perfect for our place. They were lifelong friends before joining the staff, they were friendly, and all the staff and patrons loved them. More importantly, their initial instinct in a volatile situation was to talk instead of fight. Toward the end of my career, the life of a bouncer was weighing on me heavily. I was constantly tired, and I was getting older. Seeing the effects that bar life could put on a person day in and day out took its toll, I needed a break. I drew up a schedule that would give all of us a weekend off a month. I didn't want them to experience what I had. For the first few months, I would still go to the bar but as a customer. I didn't realize it at first, but people would still come to me for issues instead of Boots, who I had put in charge on days I wasn't there. It was second nature for me to just take care of things as they came up. Boots was the kind of guy who didn't let me see it bother him, but eventually, I saw it and decided I should not come in on the nights I had off. This led to me being an ambassador to the other bars. I would find a different one to go to and hang out there with new and old friends alike. I like to sing, so I would try to find a bar that did karaoke or had a band playing. I would end up back at our place because they were open later than all the other bars, but I would have one drink and leave before closing. Usually, I would show up with a group from the other places to add to our coffers—win-win situation. I started becoming a regular at a bar in the next town over. They did karaoke on Friday nights, and many of our customers started their nights at this particular bar. I would meet some people and sing as many songs as I could. A neat feature of this place was that they had a basement bar as well as the first floor. Karaoke was downstairs, and if you didn't want to hear the *amazing* talent, you could just stay upstairs. I would split my night between both floors.

This particular Friday night, I didn't feel especially singy and decided to stay upstairs. I joined a group of people that I had befriended at a table near the door. After a while, a middle-aged man in satin pants and sport coat approached our table. I had brought a friend with me that evening, and she was attractive. When this man came over, the other girls at the table rolled their eyes. Their demeanor was that of annoyance. He slithered his way in between us, completely ignoring me, and introduced himself to my friend. She was polite and responded to him. He said he was a photographer and had never witnessed so much beauty in a single person and he would love to take her picture. My friend, who I said was polite a moment ago, was also not a sucker, laughed at him, and called him on his line. I said that I actually have beautiful eyes and he could take my picture if he wanted. He turned to face me, and I recognized the look in his eyes immediately. He was angry, and there was a hint of crazy in there. He puffed his chest out at me and went into a tirade about how he was an ex-military special forces guy that had so many confirmed kills I should be worried. I have heard this from tons of people in my years as a bouncer, and it never concerns me. I know special forces guys personally, and absolutely none of them have ever used that as an excuse to act like a clown. I made light of the situation because I didn't want there to be a problem. I apologized, and he referenced me being a female body part trying to get a rise out of me. I made eye contact with one of the bouncers, and he came over to diffuse the situation. Words were exchanged between the two, and I completely ignored him. On threat of expulsion, he left us alone for the rest of the night, but it wasn't long until he was using the same line on another group of girls. Eventually, it boiled over, and his harassment of the group of girls led to a lengthy, expletive-laden exchange that resulted in him being kicked out. All of us had a great laugh about it, and the bouncer shrugged his shoulders as if to say, "What can you do, right?" I liked this guy; he was good at his job. I turned to my group and continued having a good time.

The night carried on, and the drinks were flowing freely. The hot topic of conversation was whether I should buy a pair of silk trousers and a sport coat or not. I heard two muffled sounds and thought it was odd. I mentioned it, and the people at the table thought that maybe speakers in the karaoke room had blown. I have been around music my whole life and knew unequivocally that was not the sound I heard. I stood up from my chair because something just didn't feel right. Roughly a minute after the initial sounds, a man burst through the door. He was five feet from my group. He was dressed head to toe in camouflage. It was Silk Pants guy, but he was cosplaying as Arnold Schwarzenegger from Commando. He had shaved half his head and beard off and was brandishing a gun. He had multiple weapons on him, and as he fired his weapon into the ceiling, I dove to cover my friends. I knocked the table over and fell on top of them. He fired multiple shots into the crowd, and screams let out. He fired eight or nine shots more, took a break, and fired more. I could see people on the ground around me bleeding from gunshot wounds.

While he was administering his carnage, he kept yelling, "Where is he? WHERE THE F——K IS HE?" The place went quiet, except for the firing of the guns and the stifled screams of the injured sprawled across the floor. It was over in minutes. Some brave patrons jumped on him and were able to subdue him when he ran out of shots and was trying to reload. What had felt like hours had taken mere moments in time. No one in my group had been seriously injured by gunfire, but in the end, there were multiple casualties. Among the slain was the bouncer who had kicked him out earlier. The police arrived and questioned everyone. Ambulances and medical personnel were taking care of the wounded. The shooter was placed in a squad car and taken away. Through tear-filled eyes, my friend never let me get too far away from her. The somberness that filled the parking lot was palpable. The police came and questioned us because we had interacted with him earlier, and we recollected the story as best we could. The sun had started to crest the skyline when we were able to finally leave. I stayed with my friend that night to try and keep her at ease, but that was the start of my sleeping issues.

The reality of what had happened didn't sink in initially. Over the next week, I slowly started to comprehend what had happened. Phone calls came in hourly about the incident, and most of the questions were about the guy. Speculation on why he did it, what he looked like, what kind of gun he used, and if I was scared were all that people wanted to know. I answered them, every single time. I never told my family I was there when it happened, and that would be the beginning of the end of my career as a bouncer. Slowly, it eroded my confidence I had to keep people safe. For most of the next decade, I couldn't sleep at all without the events replaying in my dreams. Sometimes, he would shoot me; other times, he would shoot my friend, but always I never attempted to stop him. The people I was with when it happened call me a hero all the time for saving them, but I only feel like a coward. Could I have stopped him before he had the chance to fire into the crowd? He was five feet from me when he opened fire into the ceiling. Could I have stopped this lunatic from changing so many lives?

I remember having a conversation after a shooting happened when I was a kid. A question had been asked about what you would do in a situation like that if it happened. Almost every person in the circle said that they would be able to control the situation and stop it before it happened. I wasn't so confident and said I would never be in that position and wouldn't know how I would react. Well, I know the answer now. My instinct was to make sure the people I was with were safe first. Would I be able to do that again if the situation presented itself? I don't know. The important things I learned from that night are endless. I can't sit with my back to a crowd, whether at a bar or not, without anxiety coming over me. The nightmare of that incident still haunts me, not as much as before, but it is there. Now, other nightmares creep into the rotation and always with a gun and someone I care about being shot. My trust in people has vanished, and I had become a recluse until recently. From that night on, my invincibility was replaced with knowledge of my mortality. Incidents happened after that where I should have been injured or killed, but the difference now is my awareness that at any point, my decision could be my last. Almost a year to the day of the incident, I quit being a bouncer and working in the bar industry altogether. There were many reasons that led to that decision, but the most prominent one was that I no longer felt like I could provide safety in the way I used to. I was more hesitant when altercations broke out, I was less confident in my ability to talk someone down, and I was scared. I was never scared before. It all changed, this one time at a bar.

Epilogue

For a quarter of my life, I sat on a stool and watched people come and go in the bar business. I made many friends and had wonderful experiences. It defined who I was for so long that I may have lost who I was for a while. Shortly after I quit the business, I moved to a college town, and the pull to try and get a job in the business called to me hard. The money I made was fantastic, but I have nothing to show for it other than some PTSD and stories. I wouldn't change any of it for the world. Of course, I have regrets and doubts that creep in here and there, but ultimately where I am today is a direct outcome from my years as a bouncer. I learned many things about who I am and where life could take you if you make one wrong choice.

There were so many people who came in and out of our doors who all had different stories and reasons for being there. Watching people spiral downward in life because of infidelity, work, or alcoholism takes a toll on a person that I cannot completely describe. While I was living the stories, I couldn't see the adverse effect they were having on me. I was blinded by the lifestyle. It was exciting to be the guy that everyone knew. I was a celebrity in the circles that I ran in, and that was very alluring to a young man. Being invincible and the star of the show is intoxicating in its own way, and I leaned heavily into that role. Like most things in life, it eventually catches up to you, and the cracks in your armor start to show.

As much of a celebrity as I was in my chosen circle, I was a pariah in the other circles. I missed family events and hid things from my mom and dad out of fear of disappointment. Many members of my family are experiencing these stories for the first time, and for that I am sorry. I hope that those who are close to me reading this book can gain a better understanding of who, and why, I am. It was never my intention to be secretive or misleading in my lifestyle. The truth is, I was embarrassed of myself. Prior to entering the world of liquor, I had a plan on how I would leave my footprint on the world. Because of my own insecurities, I leaned heavily into a world that didn't care how smart I was. It didn't matter what I did beforehand because I was Ricky, the Door Guy. It was an amazing feeling, until it wasn't.

I realize that the end of this sounds judgy, and that isn't my intent either. It was a wonderful time, and I thank everyone who made it possible. However, there are just as many things that I witnessed that are heart-wrenching. It was an honor to do the job I did for as long as I did it. Sitting on a stool at a door for eleven years allowed me to find who I am. For that, I will eternally be grateful. These were just a handful of stories from my time in the industry. There were many more things that didn't make the cut for this round, but perhaps there will be a second, maybe third, set of them on the horizon. Enjoy life. Laugh often. Most importantly, remember to tip your bartenders! Be excellent to each other.

About the Author

Rick Jaken, hailing from a large and vibrant family, draws inspiration for his storytelling prowess from his beloved grandfather, who passed down the art of spinning captivating tales. A dedicated dog enthusiast, Rick shares his life with his Siberian husky, Loki, finding solace and adventure in their companionship. The great outdoors beckons to him, and he eagerly answers the call, immersing himself in camping and hiking expeditions.

In his moments of respite, Rick indulges in his love for literature, both as an avid reader and a wordsmith. The stories he weaves likely bear the mark of his multifaceted life experiences, enriched by the warmth of family traditions. Alongside his literary pursuits, Rick has a penchant for the imaginative realms of games like Dungeons & Dragons. Additionally, bourbon, his favorite beverage, adds a touch of sophistication to his leisurely pursuits. With a life steeped in storytelling, the outdoors, cherished family traditions, and a love for both literature and fantasy games, Rick Jaken's narrative is as diverse and rich as the worlds he explores in his writing and leisure activities.